MLOps with Red Hat OpenShift

A cloud-native approach to machine learning operations

Ross Brigoli

Faisal Masood

MLOps with Red Hat OpenShift

Group Product Manager: Niranjan Naikwadi
Publishing Product Manager: Sanjana Gupta
Book Project Manager: Hemangi Lotlikar
Senior Editor: Sushma Reddy
Technical Editor: Rahul Limbachiya
Copy Editor: Safis Editing
Proofreader: Safis Editing
Indexer: Manju Arasan
Production Designer: Prafulla Nikalje
DevRel Marketing Coordinator: Vinishka Kalra

First published: January 2024

Production reference: 1240124

Published by Packt Publishing Ltd.
Grosvenor House
11 St Paul's Square
Birmingham
B3 1RB, UK

ISBN 978-1-80512-023-0

www.packtpub.com

"To my partner in life, Hazel, for the love and support in everything that I do. To Yleana, my little genius, may these pages serve as an inspiration for your own intellectual explorations someday."

— Ross Brigoli

"To my late mother, who has supported me during my ups and downs and encouraged me to explore new horizons."

— Faisal Masood

Contributors

About the authors

Ross Brigoli is a consulting architect at Red Hat, the largest open source software company in the world, delivering innovative solutions to its customers. He has professional experience spanning more than two decades, marked by expertise in software engineering and architecture, solution design, data engineering, machine learning, DevOps, and MLOps. Before Red Hat, Ross was an associate director at Credit Agricole Corporate and Investment Bank, leading the architecture of a big data platform. Ross, along with Faisal Masood, co-authored the book *Machine Learning on Kubernetes*.

Faisal Masood is a cloud transformation architect at AWS. Faisal's focus is on assisting customers in refining and executing strategic business goals. His main interests are evolutionary architectures, software development, the ML life cycle, CD, and IaC. Faisal has over two decades of experience in software architecture and development.

About the reviewers

Baltazar Chua is a seasoned IT professional with over 20 years of diverse industry experience, including finance and telecommunications. Currently serving as a technical architect for one of Europe's leading French banks, Baltazar excels in building and designing distributed systems. His passion lies in crafting innovative solutions, showcasing a commitment to lifelong learning. Beyond his professional endeavors, Baltazar is an enthusiastic contributor to open source projects within the Cloud Native Computing Foundation and other cloud-native initiatives. In his free time, he actively supports cutting-edge solutions that drive the industry forward.

Amreth Chandrasehar is an engineering leader in cloud, AI/ML engineering, observability, and SRE. Over the last few years, Amreth has played a key role in cloud migration, generative AI, AIOps, observability, and ML adoption at various organizations. Amreth is also co-creator of Conducktor Platform, serving T-Mobile's 100+ million customers, and a tech/customer advisory board member at various companies on observability. Amreth has also co-created and open sourced Kardio.io, a service health dashboard tool. Amreth has been invited to speak at several key conferences and has won several awards.

I would like to thank my wife, Ashwinya, and my son, Athvik, for the patience and support they provided during my review of this book.

Rudrendu Kumar Paul, an AI expert and applied ML industry professional with over a decade of experience across diverse industries, excels in leading data science and engineering teams. His rich background spans multiple Fortune-50 companies in industrial applications, e-commerce, supply chain, and high-tech industries. Proficient in managing end-to-end AI and machine learning processes, he navigates experimentation, advanced analytics, and deploying models in production. Rudrendu holds an MBA, an MS in data science from Boston University, and a bachelor's in electrical engineering.

Table of Contents

Part 1: Introduction

1

Introduction to MLOps and OpenShift

Part 2: Provisioning and Configuration

2

Provisioning an MLOps Platform in the Cloud

3

Part 3: Operating ML Workloads

4

5

6

Operating ML Workloads   163

7

Building a Face Detector Using the Red Hat ML Platform   177

Index   211

Other Books You May Enjoy   218

Preface

MLOps, or **Machine Learning Operations**, is all about streamlining and harmonizing the intricate dance between developing and deploying machine learning models. It's like the conductor orchestrating a symphony, ensuring a seamless flow from the creative realm of data science to the robust reality of IT operations.

This book introduces a practical approach to implementing MLOps on the Red Hat OpenShift platform. It starts by presenting key MLOps concepts such as data preparation, model training, and packaging and deployment automation. An overview of OpenShift's fundamental building blocks—deployments, pods, and operators—is then provided. Once the basics are covered, the book delves into platform provisioning and deepens our exploration of MLOps workflows.

Throughout the book, **Red Hat OpenShift Data Science** (**RHODS**), a data science platform designed to run on OpenShift, is utilized. You will experience creating ML projects, notebooks, and training and deployment pipelines using RHODS. The book also covers the use of partner software components that complement the RHODS platform, including Pachyderm and Intel OpenVino.

By the book's end, you will gain a solid understanding of MLOps concepts, best practices, and the skills needed to implement MLOps workflows with Red Hat OpenShift Data Science on the Red Hat OpenShift platform.

Who this book is for

This book is for MLOps engineers, DevOps engineers, IT architects, and data scientists who want to gain an understanding of MLOps concepts and are interested in learning the Red Hat OpenShift Data Science platform. A basic understanding of OpenShift or Kubernetes would help in better understanding the inner workings of the exercises presented in this book. A basic knowledge of data science or machine learning and Python coding skills will also help you perform the data science parts of the exercises smoothly.

What this book covers

Chapter 1, Introduction to MLOps and OpenShift, starts with a brief introduction to MLOps and the basics of Red Hat OpenShift. The chapter then discusses how OpenShift enables machine learning projects and how Red Hat OpenShift Data Science and partner software products comprise a complete MLOPS platform.

Chapter 2, Provisioning an MLOps Platform in the Cloud, will walk you through provisioning Red Hat OpenShift, Red Hat OpenShift Data Science, and Pachyderm on the AWS cloud. The chapter contains step-by-step instructions on how to provision the base MLOps platform.

Chapter 3, Building Machine Learning Models with OpenShift, starts with the initial configurations of the platform components to prepare for model building. The chapter walks you through the configuration steps and ends with an introduction to the data science projects, workbenches, and the Jupyter Notebook.

Chapter 4, Managing a Model Training Workflow, digs deeper into the platform configuration covering OpenShift Pipelines for building model training pipelines and using Pachyderm for data versioning. By the end of the chapter, you will have built an ML model using a training pipeline you created.

Chapter 5, Deploying ML Models as a Service, introduces the model serving component of the platform. The chapter will walk you through how to enhance further the pipeline to automate the deployment of ML models.

Chapter 6, Operating ML Workloads, talks about the operational aspects of MLOps. The chapter focuses on logging and monitoring the deployed ML models and briefly discusses strategies for optimizing operational costs.

Chapter 7, Building a Face Detector Using the Red Hat ML Platform, walks you through the process of building a new AI-enabled application from end to end. The chapter helps you practice the knowledge and skills you gained in the previous chapters. The chapter also introduces Intel OpenVino as another option for model serving. By the end of this chapter, you will have built an AI-enabled web application running on OpenShift and used all of the Red Hat OpenShift Data Science features.

To get the most out of this book

You will need a basic knowledge of Kubernetes or OpenShift and basic Python coding skills on Jupyter Notebooks. Most activities are done using the web-based graphical user of Red Hat OpenShift and Red Hat OpenShift Data Science. However, specific steps require running Linux commands and interacting with the OpenShift API. Lastly, we recommend that you perform the exercises in this book to get a hands-on experience of the platform.

Software/hardware covered in the book	Operating system requirements
AWS CLI (aws)	Windows, macOS, or Linux
Red Hat OpenShift Client (oc)	Windows, macOS, or Linux

The software listed above must be installed on your local machine. These are used to interact with the platform from your client computer. The rest of the interaction with the platform is through the OpenShift web console and the Red Hat OpenShift Data Science web console.

If you are using the digital version of this book, we advise you to type the code yourself or access the code from the book's GitHub repository (a link is available in the next section). Doing so will help you avoid any potential errors related to the copying and pasting of code.

Download the example code files

You can download the example code files for this book from GitHub at `https://github.com/PacktPublishing/MLOps-with-Red-Hat-OpenShift`

If there's an update to the code, it will be updated in the GitHub repository.

We also have other code bundles from our rich catalog of books and videos available at `https://github.com/PacktPublishing/`. Check them out!

Conventions used

There are a number of text conventions used throughout this book.

`Code in text`: Indicates code words in text, database table names, folder names, filenames, file extensions, pathnames, dummy URLs, user input, and Twitter handles. Here is an example: "Create a user named `admin`."

A block of code is set as follows:

```
storage:
backend: MINIO
minio:
bucket: pachyderm
```

When we wish to draw your attention to a particular part of a code block, the relevant lines or items are set in bold:

```
curl -O -L https://mirror.openshift.com/pub/openshift-v4/client/rosa/
latest/rosa-linux.tar.gz
tar -xvzf rosa-linux.tar
echo PATH=$PATH:/home/cloudshell-user >> ~/.bashrc
```

Any command-line input or output is written as follows:

```
echo <the rendered yaml string> | oc apply -f-
```

Bold: Indicates a new term, an important word, or words that you see onscreen. For instance, words in menus or dialog boxes appear in **bold**. Here is an example: "Click on the **Increase service quotas** button if applicable to your cluster."

> **Tips or important notes**
> Appear like this.

Get in touch

Feedback from our readers is always welcome.

General feedback: If you have questions about any aspect of this book, email us at `customercare@packtpub.com` and mention the book title in the subject of your message.

Errata: Although we have taken every care to ensure the accuracy of our content, mistakes do happen. If you have found a mistake in this book, we would be grateful if you would report this to us. Please visit `www.packtpub.com/support/errata` and fill in the form.

Piracy: If you come across any illegal copies of our works in any form on the internet, we would be grateful if you would provide us with the location address or website name. Please contact us at `copyright@packt.com` with a link to the material.

If you are interested in becoming an author: If there is a topic that you have expertise in and you are interested in either writing or contributing to a book, please visit `authors.packtpub.com`.

Share Your Thoughts

Once you've read *MLOps with Red Hat OpenShift*, we'd love to hear your thoughts! Scan the QR code below to go straight to the Amazon review page for this book and share your feedback.

`https://packt.link/r/1-805-12023-9`

Your review is important to us and the tech community and will help us make sure we're delivering excellent quality content.

Download a free PDF copy of this book

Thanks for purchasing this book!

Do you like to read on the go but are unable to carry your print books everywhere?

Is your e-book purchase not compatible with the device of your choice?

Don't worry!, Now with every Packt book, you get a DRM-free PDF version of that book at no cost.

Read anywhere, any place, on any device. Search, copy, and paste code from your favorite technical books directly into your application.

The perks don't stop there, you can get exclusive access to discounts, newsletters, and great free content in your inbox daily

Follow these simple steps to get the benefits:

1. Scan the QR code or visit the following link:

https://packt.link/free-ebook/9781805120230

2. Submit your proof of purchase.
3. That's it! We'll send your free PDF and other benefits to your email directly.

Part 1:
Introduction

This part covers the basic concepts of MLOps and an introduction to Red Hat OpenShift.

This part has the following chapters:

- *Chapter 1, Introduction to MLOps and OpenShift*

1

Introduction to MLOps and OpenShift

If you have chosen to read this book, chances are that you have a background in the **machine learning** (**ML**) domain. The primary purpose of this book is to show you how Red Hat OpenShift provides the basis for developing, deploying, and monitoring your models in production. In addition, you will learn about different components of the OpenShift ecosystem and how you can weave them together to build a path toward automating the life cycle of your ML project. You will also learn how to leverage Red Hat OpenShift Data Science and its partner components.

Finally, you will see how the approaches presented in this book can help your organization scale its ML initiatives through MLOps practices.

This first chapter focuses on giving you the basic definitions of the concepts and the technologies involved in the Red Hat OpenShift ecosystem for machine learning.

This chapter will cover the following topics:

- What is **machine learning operations** (**MLOps**)?
- Introduction to OpenShift
- How OpenShift enables you to implement MLOps
- The advantages of the cloud

Let's start by defining MLOps.

What is MLOps?

MLOps is a set of practices that aims to streamline the process of deploying and maintaining ML models in production environments. It involves integrating ML workflows with DevOps practices to ensure that ML models are tested, deployed, and monitored in a reliable and scalable manner.

MLOps involves collaboration between data scientists, ML engineers, software developers, and operations teams to create a continuous integration and delivery pipeline for ML models. This pipeline includes steps such as data preparation, model training, model testing, model deployment, and monitoring. MLOps also involves the use of automation, testing, and monitoring tools to ensure that models remain accurate, stable, and scalable over time.

Some common practices in MLOps include version control for models and data, experiment tracking, model validation, continuous integration and delivery, containerization of models, and monitoring of model performance and data drift.

So, what problems does MLOps aim to solve? ML is still an emerging domain, and as per a Gartner study, 53% of projects fail to move from prototypes to production. The primary reasons include the model development life cycle, operationalization of models, and overall workflow governance. MLOps takes learnings from proven software engineering practices, such as DevOps, and applies them to ML projects.

MLOps is an emerging domain that takes advantage of the maturity of existing software development processes – in other words, DevOps combined with data engineering and ML disciplines. MLOps can be simply defined as an engineering practice of applying DevOps to ML projects.

Let's look at how these disciplines form the foundation of MLOps.

First, unlike traditional programming, where your only input is the code written by the developers, in ML, your input is both code and data. While the application package is the output of the application build process in software engineering, in ML, the written code is only used to facilitate the training of a known algorithm using a training dataset. The behavior of the resulting ML model is highly dependent on the training dataset, the algorithm, and the code used to perform the training. As a result, even if you do not change your code and use a different dataset, the resulting ML model may perform differently. This adds another layer of complexity as this requires not only versioning the code that facilitates model training but also versioning the training dataset for a repeatable outcome. Versioning data requires a different approach compared to versioning code. This is because we generally don't want to store multiple versions of the entire dataset inside a Git repository. One method is to take the hash of the data and then apply Git-like practices to keep a history of changes. This allows us to avoid storing multiple versions of the entire dataset inside the Git repository. You will see how Pachyderm, a component available on the OpenShift platform, provides such capabilities.

Secondly, an ML project involves more personas than a traditional software project. You have data scientists, ML engineers, and data engineers collaborating with software engineers, business analysts or subject matter experts, and platform and operations teams. Sometimes, these personas are very diverse. For example, a data scientist may not wholly understand the production deployment process of a model. Similarly, the operations team may not fully understand what a model is. Later in this book, you will see how the OpenShift platform provides a way to automate the process of packaging and deploying models for inference with tools such as Intel OpenVino.

Third, unlike traditional software development, where you only need to develop one working code set, in ML, a data scientist or ML engineer may use multiple ML algorithms and generate multiple resulting ML models. In other words, they perform experiments on different types of algorithms and different ways of training, and they use different sets of dataset features. Before selecting a model fit for production, your team needs to compare different dimensions of the model before choosing one. MLOps tackles this additional dimension of the workflow by providing tools to version and compare model performances. MLflow is one such tool that allows to manage experiments and it runs on OpenShift. By using MLflow, we can demonstrate that we can always extend the toolset to fit our needs.

Training an ML algorithm to produce an ML model can take hours or days, sometimes weeks, especially when you use complex **deep learning** (**DL**) algorithms. This kind of training process may require a different set of hardware, such as GPUs and memory-optimized machines. You will see how OpenShift and the cloud assist in automating the availability to optimize cost and training time. In addition, OpenShift's capability for scaling resources during inference helps with meeting production SLAs.

Lastly, because ML models' performances rely on the dataset used during training, if this dataset no longer represents the real-world situation, the model's effectiveness may degrade. This will result in inaccurate responses and reduced value for the user. This is called model drift. Early drift detection keeps the model relevant and functional, allowing it to continually deliver value for the business. OpenShift provides a way to not only capture traditional metrics, such as response times, but can also be extended to detect model drifts.

Because of the complexity ML adds compared to traditional programming, the need to address these complexities led to the emergence of MLOps. As a result, Red Hat has packaged a set of components that provides MLOps capabilities for the OpenShift platform. It is called **Red Hat OpenShift Data Science** or **RHODS** (pronounced "rhodes").

This book covers the elements of the RHODS offering and partner components on the OpenShift platform for a complete MLOps solution.

Let's start by refreshing our understanding of the OpenShift platform.

Introduction to OpenShift

Although this book is not about operationalizing the OpenShift platform, a basic introduction to the platform is helpful. In this section, you will learn about the core concepts of Kubernetes and OpenShift.

OpenShift is a complete application platform based on Kubernetes. It is also categorized as Enterprise Kubernetes. Kubernetes provides a solid foundation for container hosting and orchestration. Moreover, Kubernetes provides core functionalities, such as cluster-state management, where a reconcile loop makes sure that the cluster state and the desired state are in sync. Kubernetes also includes a set of APIs to interact with the cluster. Kubernetes is a great platform, but in reality, applications need much more than just the core services provided by Kubernetes.

Assume that you want to deploy a Python application on a Kubernetes cluster. Let's assess what is required. First, you need to package your application as a container image. Secondly, you must store this container image in an image registry. Your application may need a backend service such as a cache or a database. You may need to call other services from your application. You will need to monitor your application and may be required to generate alerts of critical events. All these things are needed to make your application ready for production. A complete application platform, such as OpenShift, answers all these concerns. OpenShift enhances the Kubernetes platform to enhance the support of application life cycles, operations, and security. OpenShift is available on all the major clouds and on-premises, via which you can consistently deploy your workloads across multiple cloud providers and hybrid environments.

OpenShift has all the functionalities of a vanilla Kubernetes platform with additions such as developer-centric toolsets that make it easier for developers and ML engineers to build, deploy, and manage containerized applications.

OpenShift is available in several different editions. **OpenShift Container Platform** is the on-premises version of OpenShift that can be installed on either bare-metal or virtualized infrastructure. **OpenShift Dedicated** is a fully managed OpenShift cluster managed by Red Hat. You can gain access to it through a Red Hat subscription. **Red Hat OpenShift on AWS (ROSA)** is an AWS offering of OpenShift. It is fully managed jointly by AWS and Red Hat. **Azure Red Hat OpenShift (ARO)** is an Azure Cloud offering of OpenShift. It is fully managed jointly by Microsoft and Red Hat. **OpenShift Kubernetes Engine** is an OpenShift offering on the Google Cloud platform. There are other flavors of OpenShift and different types of OpenShift subscriptions. Among them are **Red Hat OpenShift on IBM Cloud**, **OpenShift Platform Plus**, which includes **Red Hat ACM**, **Advanced Cluster Security (ACS)**, **Data Foundation**, and **Red Hat Quay**. **Single-Node OpenShift (SNO)** is also available for deployments to the edge. Each edition is designed to meet the specific needs of different types of users, from individual developers to large enterprise organizations. One of the strengths of OpenShift is that regardless of where and which infrastructure OpenShift is running, the developer experience remains consistent, making it easy to move your workloads across different infrastructures without impacting the platform's end users.

Overall, OpenShift is a powerful platform for running and managing modern containerized applications in both on-premises and cloud environments. It is an enterprise-grade Kubernetes distribution that's loaded with many additional features that focus on improving the developer experience.

Kubernetes resources

Now that you have a basic understanding of what OpenShift is, we also think it is beneficial for you to refresh yourself on some of the basic concepts of Kubernetes. Most of the critical components and resources of OpenShift and Kubernetes platform that you need to understand are as follows:

- **Cluster**: A cluster is a general name for a group of computers that work together to form a single computing platform. In the context of this book, a cluster refers to a Kubernetes cluster. We will also use this term interchangeably to refer to OpenShift clusters. A cluster has two sets of host servers – the control plane nodes and the compute nodes. They are often referred to as master nodes and worker nodes, respectively. The control plane manages all of the resources in a cluster. It also hosts all of the containers that run the core components of Kubernetes, including the Kubernetes API. The compute nodes, on the other hand, are the nodes in a cluster that host the rest of the application workloads and are managed by the control plane. The Kubernetes scheduler that runs in the control plane decides what compute node your container lands on, making sure the load of the worker nodes is balanced. This process is called container orchestration. The actual orchestration algorithm is much more complex than what is defined here, but this definition is enough to help you understand how Kubernetes works with containers.

- **Container**: A container is a standard way of packaging your code, its dependencies, configuration, and parts of the operating system into a Linux container. Containers run as processes in the host operating system, sharing the Linux kernel with the host through a container runtime. Different Kubernetes distributions use different container runtimes. The most recent version of Kubernetes uses a container runtime, which adheres to **Container Runtime Interface** (**CRI**) standards. CRI defines the set of specifications via which kubelet integrates with the runtime. OpenShift uses CRI-O as its container runtime. **CRI-O** is an implementation of the CRI for **Open Container Initiative** (**OCI**) runtimes. It is a lightweight alternative to **Docker**.

> **Note**
>
> Standardizing application packages provides the capability to run the application packages on any host operating system that has an OCI-compatible container runtime. Additionally, containers allow for the standardization of operations such as loading, unloading, and mounting persistent storage. This allows both the development and operations teams to use a common artifact when dealing with deployments, regardless of the application framework used. That common artifact is called the container image.

- **Container image**: A container image, sometimes referred to as an **image**, is a static executable package file that contains the definition of a container. A container image, when executed, creates an instance of the container. Container images are created by compiling or building a container definition file, more commonly known as a **Dockerfile**, which contains the specifics of what should be packaged and executed inside a container. This definition includes the operating system in the form of a **base image**, the application to run, its dependencies, and any configuration required by the resulting container. To put it simply, when a Dockerfile is built, it creates a container image. When the container image is executed, it creates an instance of the container.

- **Base image**: A base image is a container image that's used as a basis for creating another container image. This is defined inside the Dockerfile using the **FROM** keyword. When building a Dockerfile from a certain base image, the resulting container image inherits all the properties of the base image plus the additional properties and packages added on top of it. Base images usually come from a repository of container images called an image registry.

- **Namespace**: Namespaces are a way to logically divide your cluster resources into separate isolated spaces to manage your cluster and user accesses better. This is very useful if your cluster is multi-tenant – that is, multiple teams are sharing the cluster. Each namespace is isolated in terms of resource namings and DNS. You can think of namespaces as virtual clusters within the Kubernetes cluster.

> **Note**
>
> In OpenShift, we do not deal directly with namespaces. OpenShift uses projects, which encapsulate a Kubernetes namespace and add additional attributes to it. Any changes we make to a project implicitly change the underlying namespace.

- **Pod**: A pod is the smallest unit of deployment in a Kubernetes cluster and can contain one or many containers. Containers in a pod share the same IP address and, optionally, share the storage volumes. The idea is to allow all the containers within a pod to communicate more efficiently. Typically, you should only have one main container that runs your application inside a pod. The other containers within the same pod as your application usually act as helpers. For example, you may have containers that prepare the database by inserting data into the database before your application starts. These are called **initContainers**. Another example is that you may need to create a helper container that monitors your application or serves as a reverse proxy for your main application container. This is called a **sidecar container**.

- **Deployment**: A deployment contains the specifications for deploying an application workload through pods. It manages the instances of pods for a specific application workload. It also maintains the number of replicas of the pod through a **ReplicaSet**. Deployment is the main entry point for deploying applications within Kubernetes and OpenShift. It contains the definition of pods, the storage volumes that need to be mounted, the service account to be used, the environment variables, and much more.

- **DeploymentConfig**: DeploymentConfig is an OpenShift-specific construct for defining deployments, similar to the Deployment object. DeploymentConfig has specific features that deployments do not have in that it provides automatic rollbacks to the last successfully deployed ReplicaSet in case of a failure. DeploymentConfigs also require the explicit rollout of applications, adding more control as to when to rollout changes.

- **ReplicaSet**: A ReplicaSet ensures that the number of pod replicas is correct as per the desired state. It is responsible for spinning up new copies of pods and killing pods when the number of running pods is less than the configured number of replicas. We usually do not manage ReplicaSets directly as they are managed by deployments.

- **StatefulSets**: StatefulSets are very similar to deployments. However, they are meant for deploying stateful applications. StatefulSets maintain the stickyness of pod identities, including their hostnames across the pod's life cycle. StatefulSets also ensure that the sequence of pod startups is done in a way that they do not overlap with another running copy of the pod. These are usually used for deploying distributed databases or applications that require pod clustering, such as Redis and Elasticsearch.

- **DaemonSets**: DaemonSets are also very similar to Deployment and StatefulSets. It manages instances of pods. However, DaemonSets ensure that there is always one copy of the pod running for each worker node. This is typically used for system-level pods such as logging and monitoring.

- **Service**: Pods are ephemeral. They can be destroyed and created by a Kubernetes scheduler from time to time. Every time they are created, they may have a different name. A service serves as a logical grouping of pods that exposes the pods to the Kubernetes network. A service also serves as the load balancer to deployments with multiple pod replicas. A service has an IP address and an internal domain name that can be accessed within the Kubernetes cluster.

- **Ingress**: An ingress is a Kubernetes object that manages external access to services. It also provides SSL termination and load balancing capabilities when it is pointing to more than one service.

- **Route**: Similar to ingresses, a route is a reverse proxy that exposes services as external APIs, typically over HTTP. It also provides SSL termination and load balancing capabilities. Routes are OpenShift-only objects and are not available in vanilla Kubernetes by default.

- **Custom resources (CRs)**: CRs allow us to extend the capabilities of Kubernetes. On top of the built-in resources we covered previously, we can add CRs that perform a specific functionality while encapsulating the built-in resources. CRs are created through a built-in resource called a **custom resource definition (CRD)**. Instead of interacting with deployments, pods, services, and other resources, a CR can encapsulate the operations that are tailored to the particular service that you want to create.

- **CRD**: Extending Kubernetes means creating CRDs. A CRD is what we use to define a new kind of object or resource in Kubernetes. This new object is called a CRD and is typically managed by Operators. You will learn about operators later.

The objects and terms that we have described so far are the key Kubernetes and OpenShift objects that we will be dealing with as users of OpenShift. Since OpenShift is based on Kubernetes, all these components are available in the OpenShift platform. Let's see what additional components OpenShift provides to make it a complete application platform.

OpenShift features

The following concepts, features, and practices also come with OpenShift and are important to be familiar with.

- **Cluster life cycle management**: OpenShift can automatically update the cluster and notify you when an update is available. OpenShift supports canary updates for controlled updates for the worker nodes. This is done through cluster operators.

- **Advanced Cluster Security** (**ACS**): Red Hat ACS is an optional add-on feature from OpenShift that provides cloud-native security. You can integrate ACS with CI/CD pipelines and image registries to provide continuous scanning for your applications. ACS also scans your Kubernetes infrastructure against security benchmarks such as the **Center for Internet Security** (**CIS**). ACS is based on *StackRox*, an open source Kubernetes-native security platform.

- **Advanced Cluster Management** (**ACM**): Red Hat ACM is another add-on feature in OpenShift that allows you to centrally manage multiple Kubernetes clusters, regardless of where they are running. This helps the operations team in managing multiple Kubernetes and OpenShift clusters. This also allows workloads to be moved from one cluster to another. Red Hat ACM is based on **Open Cluster Management** (**OCM**), an open source multi-cloud and multicluster solution.

- **Image registry**: An image registry or image repository, sometimes referred to as a registry, is a repository of container images. **Docker Hub** is the most well-known image registry on the internet. An image registry behaves like a Git repository of container images. You can store and fetch images to and from a registry and share your images with others who want to use your published images. Modern registries provide additional capabilities, such as container vulnerability scanning of images stored in the registry, for additional security.

- OpenShift has an integrated image registry to manage container images within the cluster. Being a complete platform, OpenShift can build, deploy, and store container images from source code using its built-in pipelines and internal container registry. There are also other image registries that you will work with throughout this book. This includes **Quay.io** and **Red Hat Catalog**.

- **Monitoring**: OpenShift includes a prepackaged monitoring stack for all the core platform components of OpenShift. The same logging technology stack can be configured to monitor application workloads within OpenShift. The monitoring stack uses **Prometheus** and **Grafana** to collect, store, and visualize events and telemetry data.

- **Logging**: OpenShift also provides a prepackaged system where application logging stack cluster logs, applications, and infrastructure logs are aggregated. You can store these logs in the default log store or forward them to your enterprise log store. The logging stack uses **Elasticsearch, FluentD, and Kibana** (**EFK**) to collect, store, query, and visualize logs, respectively.

- **GitOps**: GitOps helps implement continuous deployment for cloud-native applications. It can also be used to manage OpenShift cluster components such as operators. OpenShift GitOps is based on ArgoCD.

- **CI/CD**: GitOps is just one component of the CI/CD process. OpenShift has Tekton pipelines to build, test, validate, and package applications on the platform.

Figure 1.1 shows the additional capabilities that OpenShift adds on top of Kubernetes to form a complete application platform:

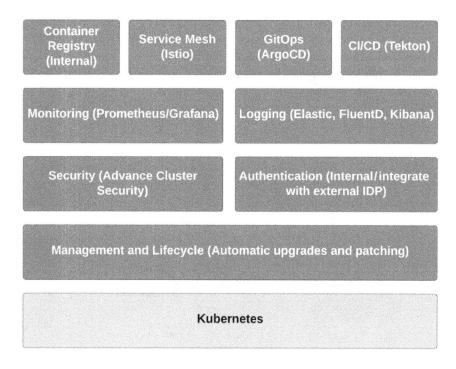

Figure 1.1 – OpenShift's added features

As you may have already understood, OpenShift is a Kubernetes distribution that adds several capabilities to Kubernetes that allow containerized applications to be managed much easier. Why is this important? Because all of the MLOps components we'll introduce in this book are applications. OpenShift enables us to run these applications consistently, reliably, and securely.

Another important feature of OpenShift is **operator life cycle management**. This feature allows you to deploy operators that can manage services for you. For the components that your application depends on, such as databases and monitoring, OpenShift simplifies provisioning and running them via operators.

So, let's take some time to understand operators.

Understanding operators

In traditional organizations, specialized and dedicated teams were required to maintain applications and other software components such as databases, caches, and messaging components. Moreover, those teams were continuously observing the software ecosystem and doing specific things, such as taking backups for databases, upgrading and patching newer versions of software components, and more.

Operators in Kubernetes are like system administrators or human operators, continuously monitoring applications running on the Kubernetes environment and performing operational tasks associated with the specific component. In summary, an operator extends Kubernetes to automate the management of the complete life cycle of an application. For example, a PostgreSQL operator automates the database's high availability, installation, patching, and backup abilities, to name a few. Many operators are available for various software components, such as databases, caches, and queues, from Red Hat Catalog and software partners.

Figure 1.2 shows how an operator automates operational activities. In the traditional approach, a developer develops the application, and then the operations team provides support to run the application. In contrast, the Kubernetes operator aims to automate the operational activities to minimize human intervention in running and operating the applications in production. This not only reduces the amount of work required from the system administrator but also eliminates human errors:

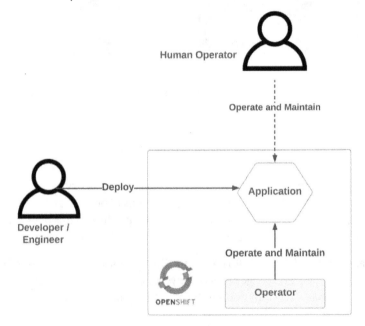

Figure 1.2 – Operators in OpenShift

Operators can also be configured to perform version upgrades automatically or manually. When the operator is configured for manual upgrade, a notification is sent to a designated recipient, typically a platform engineer or a systems administrator, where they can trigger the upgrade manually. The actual upgrade operation is still performed by the operator, thus eliminating human errors in the process.

OpenShift has a rich ecosystem of operators that you can install through the Operator Hub. The Operator Hub can be accessed directly from the OpenShift web console, as shown in *Figure 1.3*, much like the App Store. It is a marketplace for Kubernetes operators, ranging from open source community-supported ones to Red Hat-certified operators and commercially-supported ones:

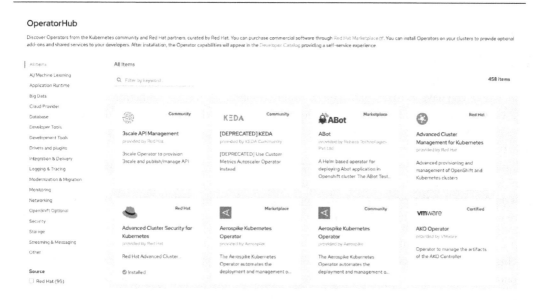

Figure 1.3 – Operator Hub in the OpenShift console

It is important to understand operators because the primary software components that form the MLOps platform on OpenShift are delivered as operators.

In the next section, we'll understand the advantages of running and implementing MLOps in OpenShift.

Understanding how OpenShift supports MLOps

As you have seen, an application platform provides an opinionated way of running services on Kubernetes. An example of this is OpenShift, which provides Prometheus and Grafana as monitoring services. A similar approach is applied to the software required to run MLOps on OpenShift. Red Hat and its partners provide MLOps components on top of the OpenShift platform that provides the services for a complete ML platform. Using OpenShift, all the MLOps capabilities can be consistently deployed on-premises and on the cloud.

Just like DevOps, one of the primary objectives of MLOps is to bridge the gap between the engineers who are building the applications – or in this case, the data scientists and ML engineers who are developing ML models – and the operations team. To achieve this, we need to have a common platform where engineers and operators will meet. The best tool we have for this is containerization platforms. This allows both operations and engineering teams to use a common language when dealing with deployments. However, a containerization platform alone is not enough when it comes to ML projects – there are additional gaps that need to be addressed. For example, data scientists are often not software engineers and have limited knowledge in packaging and deploying containerized applications compared to developers. This is where it is important to abstract and automate the packaging of ML models into intelligent applications. This can be done through model serving, which can be automated within OpenShift.

Another important step in the ML project life cycle is model development. This task often requires significant compute resources. Oftentimes, we have seen data scientists using their own laptop or desktop computers to train models. This is fine for simple ML models, but it is not practical for huge neural networks trained with huge datasets. The best option for training such models is to go to the cloud, where you have virtually unlimited compute resources. However, sometimes, you don't have the luxury of bringing your dataset to the cloud for reasons such as data privacy, data sovereignty, and other regulatory restrictions. In this case, you will be using your own data center to train your models. This is where OpenShift plays a vital role. Being a hybrid cloud platform, it allows you to run multiple OpenShift clusters both on your data center and in the cloud. This allows you to run model training tasks that use sensitive data on your data center while running the rest of the model training tasks on the cloud without having to learn a new set of tools. OpenShift also allows you to seamlessly move workloads across different clusters through advanced cluster management.

With OpenShift, data scientists can take advantage of the unlimited compute power of the cloud instead of being restricted by the compute resources of their laptop computers. OpenShift comes with a GPU operator that allows pods to use GPU compute resources on the host servers of your OpenShift cluster.

GPT-3, the language model that powers ChatGPT, was trained using 285,000 CPU cores and 10,000 Nvidia GPUs on Azure Cloud. You probably do not have this amount of resources in your entire data center, but the cloud has this.

OpenShift alone brings many benefits to ML workloads. However, to further improve the support for ML projects on OpenShift, Red Hat released an operator called RHODS.

Red Hat OpenShift Data Science (RHODS)

In this section, you will explore the components that form the ML platform stack. The technology stack is a combination of Red Hat components, Red Hat partner components, and open source software. It's called RHODS, and it's Red Hat's solution for running data science and ML workloads on OpenShift.

Running RHODS on OpenShift gives the freedom to build and deploy models on-premises or on any cloud. The open source version of RHODS is **Open Data Hub** (`https://opendatahub.io`). RHODS provides a subset of the components available in Open Data Hub but in a commercially supported way. The RHODS platform integrates well with technology partners to form a complete MLOps stack.

You will learn about the RHODS platform throughout this book. Let's start by defining some of its building blocks:

- **Model development and tuning**: RHODS provides out-of-the-box support for **JupyterHub**, a powerful and popular multi-user Jupyter notebook server. It provides a central hub for creating and managing **JupyterLab** notebooks on Kubernetes and OpenShift. The JupyterHub platform ships with pre-packaged container images with common Python libraries and packages such as **TensorFlow** and **PyTorch**. The platform allows users to easily build containers; you will build some in the following chapters. The platform uses a Kubeflow notebook controller to manage multiple notebooks.

You can also use the Anaconda Red Hat OpenShift Data Science platform.

- **Data management**: RHODS utilizes partners to provide data management capabilities. **Trino**, which runs on the platform, provides federated query facilities to a variety of data sources such as streaming, relational, and unstructured files using standard SQL. Trino runs the query in a distributed fashion to provide the speed and scale for your data needs. The commercial product for Trino is **Starburst**. It's certified to run on OpenShift and is available as a commercially supported, vendor-managed component on top of OpenShift. You will deploy Trino and use it to run queries and analytics in the following chapters.

- **Data storage**: Though Trino can pull data from a variety of sources, an MLOps platform provides scalable storage to adhere to its storage requirements. OpenShift Data Foundation is the scalable storage offering for the platform. The platform can also utilize cloud storage options, such as S3. In this book, you will use the open source Minio component running on top of OpenShift to provide a scalable S3-compatible store.

- **Data ingestion**: You can write code to ingest data using Python on a Jupyter notebook. The platform provides **Red Hat OpenShift Streams for Apache Kafka**, a component based on open source Kafka that can be used to ingest data into the platform. Red Hat OpenShift Streams for Kafka is offered as a fully managed service on the cloud. **Red Hat AMQ Streams** provides the same functionality but can be self-managed and installed via the Operator Hub.

- **GPU**: When it comes to training models, hardware resources such as GPUs can speed up this task and help reduce the model development time. GPUs are expensive resources and teams should share the GPUs as needed. RHODS allows you to associate a GPU with a notebook; once the job is done, the same GPU resources can be released and allocated to another user's notebook in the organization. Combine this with the cloud's ability to provision and destroy resources on-demand and you get a flexible and cost-optimized way of using GPUs. You will see how RHODS enables you to request GPU resources with ease later in this book.

There are more advanced options such as virtualizing a single physical GPU into multiple virtual GPUs via the software for even more fine-grained GPU sharing, and there are technology partners such as **run.ai** that provide a complete platform to optimize the utilization of your GPUs. GPU-sharing topics are outside the scope of this book, but you will receive pointers in the following chapters if you want to explore this capability further.

- **Model serving and observability**: Model serving is the process of packaging your ML model into an application that can be accessed via an API. Packaging models can be done manually, but as mentioned earlier, data scientists and ML engineers may not necessarily know how to write applications that expose an ML model as an API. Because of this, it is vital to automate the process of packaging and serving ML models.

  Once you have built your model, it will be packaged and deployed as a container on the Red Hat OpenShift platform. You will also learn how to package and tune the model for inferencing using tools such as **Seldon and Intel OpenVINO**. You will see how to use the OpenVINO model server to deploy models and capture metrics. These metrics are Prometheues-compatible and integrate well with the OpenShift monitoring stack.

You can see all these components in *Figure 1.4*. We will not be able to demonstrate the use of other commercial third-party software and cloud services. This is to give you an idea of where RHODS sits in the ecosystem and what other components can be added to your MLOps platform:

> **Note**
>
> You are not limited to the software and services shown in *Figure 1.4*. You can add other third-party software and services to your OpenShift cluster, so long as they are supported or run on OpenShift.

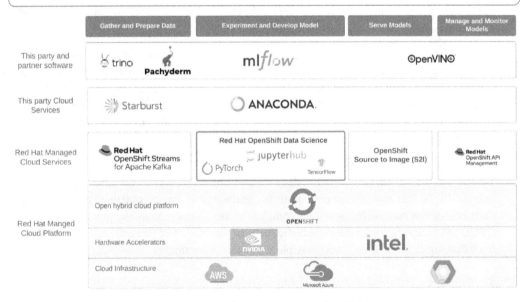

Figure 1.4 – Red Hat ecosystem with RHODS

To summarize, OpenShift's DevOps capabilities offer a powerful platform for accelerating the delivery of AI-powered applications and streamlining the integration and redeployment of ML models to enhance prediction accuracy. By extending OpenShift's DevOps automation capabilities to the ML life cycle, data scientists, software developers, and IT operations professionals can collaborate more effectively to integrate ML models into the development of intelligent applications. This approach enhances productivity, simplifies life cycle management for ML-powered intelligent applications, and offers a range of advanced features, including a container images registry with OpenShift Build, continuous iterative development of ML model-powered intelligent applications with OpenShift Pipelines, continuous deployment automation for ML models powered by intelligent applications with OpenShift GitOps, and an image repository to version model container images and microservices with Red Hat Quay.

The advantages of the cloud

Cloud computing provides on-demand delivery of IT resources such as servers, networks, storage, databases, and all higher-level application services via the internet with a pay-as-you-go pricing model. The prominent vendors for the cloud are **Amazon Web Services** (**AWS**), Microsoft Azure, and Google Cloud, and they all provide usage-based pricing.

The cloud has many benefits, but the top three are agility, innovation, and cost savings. Let's take a brief look at all three.

Agility ensures that the teams can experiment with new ideas quickly and frequently. That's because the speed your team can deliver software is higher when the team doesn't wait for IT to provision infrastructure. This makes the foundation of autonomous product teams, where they can release products, collect feedback, and improve the software to meet your customers' needs.

Agility powers your team to focus on business competence instead of using the time to manage IT infrastructure. Cloud is growing tremendously while providing new service abstraction for you. One such example is serverless, where you don't need to worry about infrastructure. This provides the basis for teams to innovate and perform higher-value work within the organization. You will see how using OpenShift on the cloud simplifies management and scaling for you so that you can focus on business outcomes.

Lastly, because you only pay for what you use, it results in cost savings compared to traditional data centers. This is not always true, though; if you treat the cloud as yet another data center, you may end up paying higher than you would for a traditional data center. You may need to rethink and redesign your systems so that they use the variable billing of the cloud and move to higher-level services such as serverless instead of running a virtual machine instance in the cloud to find the savings. You will see how OpenShift machine sets allow for an elastic infrastructure and provide the technical foundation for you to save costs.

OpenShift provides an abstraction layer for your team to run containers on any cloud and/or on-premises data center. We discussed all these services in the *Understanding how OpenShift supports MLOps* section.

We are using AWS as our cloud; you can choose whatever cloud is more accessible for you. OpenShift is available on all three clouds, and AWS and Azure provide a managed offering for OpenShift, namely ROSA and ARO.

ROSA

ROSA is a fully managed turnkey application platform that enables you to focus on delivering value to your customers. ROSA is a service operated by Red Hat and jointly supported with AWS to provide a fully managed OpenShift platform. Red Hat and AWS teams work on the underlying infrastructure for you to reduce the burden of managing infrastructure. ROSA also includes integration with a wide range of AWS services, such as databases and mobile, to help you further accelerate building solutions for your organization.

The following are some of the benefits of the ROSA platform:

- If you are running OpenShift on-premises, ROSA provides the fastest path to running OpenShift in the cloud. ROSA provides production-ready OpenShift as a service on the AWS platform.

- Red Hat and AWS jointly operate and support ROSA. This provides an integrated support channel for you with a 99.95% uptime. (The 99.95% uptime is quoted from the vendor's site and may change).

- ROSA provides pay-as-you-go pricing with hourly and annual billing. This provides flexibility for you to choose as per your business needs.

We do not favor any specific cloud offerings and will continue to use OpenShift as our baseline to build our MLOps stack. However, ROSA has been mentioned here to show you the benefits of a managed service. We will also be using ROSA as the OpenShift platform to run the exercises in this book.

Summary

In this chapter, you learned about the problems MLOps aims to tackle and how it can increase the velocity of your data science initiatives. You also refreshed your knowledge of Kubernetes and OpenShift and saw how Red Hat OpenShift provides a consistent and reliable environment where you can run your container workloads on-premises and in the cloud. You have seen how RHODS, using the strengths of the underlying container platform, provides a full set of components for an MLOps platform.

In the next chapter, you will learn about the stages of the ML life cycle, as well as the role MLOps plays in implementing all the stages of model development and deployment. You will also see how teams collaborate during model development and deployment stages and how RHODS components relate to each stage of the ML life cycle.

References

To learn more about the topics that were covered in this chapter, take a look at the following resources:

- Gartner identifies AI Engineering as a top trend for 2021 and beyond. `https://www.gartner.com/en/newsroom/press-releases/2020-10-19-gartner-identifies-the-top-strategic-technology-trends-for-2021`

- MLflow, an open-source tool, supports model versioning, deployment, and sharing model performance data. `https://mlflow.org`

- Trino, an open-source distributed query engine, facilitates fetching data from diverse sources for model training. `https://trino.io`

- Run.ai offers certified software for pooling and sharing GPU resources, addressing the cost challenges of training models. `https://www.run.ai/`

- OpenVINO optimizes models for Intel-based hardware, from data centers to edge devices like IoT devices and phones. `https://docs.openvino.ai/latest/home.html`

Part 2: Provisioning and Configuration

This part covers preparing the cloud environment, provisioning and configuring Red Hat OpenShift and Red Hat OpenShift Data Science, and integrating the platform components. This part also covers the initial platform configuration required for building ML models.

This part has the following chapters:

- *Chapter 2, Provisioning an MLOps Platform in the Cloud*
- *Chapter 3, Building Machine Learning Models with OpenShift*

2

Provisioning an MLOps Platform in the Cloud

Now that you have an understanding of MLOps and the different stages of a **machine learning** (**ML**) life cycle, in this chapter, you will provision a managed Red Hat OpenShift cluster on the **Amazon Web Services** (**AWS**) cloud. You will then provision Red Hat **OpenShift Data Science** (**ODS**) and partner components on the Red Hat OpenShift platform.

The focus of this chapter is to provide you with an overview of how to build your MLOps platform using OpenShift and a cloud vendor. The agility of Red Hat OpenShift paired with cloud services provides a solid foundation for you to build your MLOps platform in very little time. Keep in mind that the OpenShift platform is cloud-agnostic, and you can use it with your on-premises infrastructure if this is the path you want to take.

This chapter does not make you an expert in provisioning the OpenShift platform. There are many books and tons of documentation providing such details, and we leave it to you to consult them. This chapter will cover the following topics:

- Installing OpenShift on AWS
- Installing Red Hat ODS
- Installing partner software on Red Hat ODS

Let's start with the provisioning of a basic ROSA cluster.

Technical requirements

You will need a computer with internet access to provision the platform in AWS. You will also need an active AWS account, which you will use to create the resources required by the platform. You should have basic knowledge of interacting with the AWS portal.

Installing OpenShift on AWS

Red Hat OpenShift Service on AWS (ROSA) is a fully managed Red Hat OpenShift platform. ROSA is operated and supported jointly by AWS and Red Hat. With ROSA, you move your focus from managing infrastructure to managing applications and bringing more business value to your organization. ROSA provides an integrated experience for OpenShift cluster creation, a pay-as-you-go (hourly and annual) billing, and a single invoice for AWS deployments. ROSA helps to reduce operational complexity with automated deployment and management, backed by a global Red Hat **site reliability engineering (SRE)** team.

The workflow for ROSA creation involves many steps. The setup defined here shows you the steps involved in an easy way and for learning purposes. The settings provided here are not recommended for production clusters.

> **Note**
>
> In a production setup, you will need to integrate the platform with your own **identity provider (IdP)**. You may need to configure firewalls to limit access to your cluster, and you may want to set up for **disaster recovery (DR)**.

We broke down the installation process into the following three main stages:

- Prepare AWS accounts and service quotas
- Enable ROSA and register for a Red Hat account
- Install ROSA

Let's see what is involved in each of these stages.

Preparing AWS accounts and service quotas

We assume that you have an AWS account already available. ROSA requires a dedicated **Identity and Access Management (IAM)** account to be used for provisioning the OpenShift cluster. The first stage is to create another IAM account, which you will use to create a ROSA cluster:

1. Log in to the AWS console and search for the **IAM** service, as shown in *Figure 2.1*:

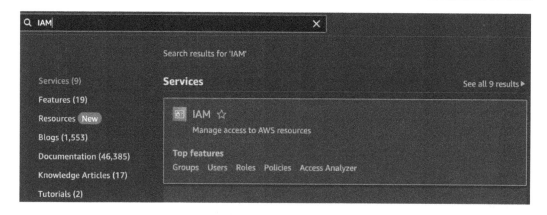

Figure 2.1 – Searching for IAM in the AWS console

2. Select **Users** on the left menu and click on the **Add users** button on the right-hand side:

Figure 2.2 – Adding a new user to IAM

3. Create a user named `admin`. Check the *console* access for this user and set the password. Click **Next**:

Figure 2.3 – IAM user creation in the AWS console

4.   In the **Set permissions** page, select **AdministratorAccess** under the **Attach policies directly** radio button. Note that this setting provides a relaxed policy and should not be used for the production cluster. Click **Next**:

Figure 2.4 – AWS user creation permission options

5. In the last step, select **Create user**. Although we have not added any tags, it is highly recommended that you add tags as per your cloud policy:

Figure 2.5 – AWS console user creation review page

6. As a best practice, select the user that you just created, select the **Security Credentials** tab, and add a **multi-factor authentication** (**MFA**) device by clicking the **Assign MFA device** button:

Figure 2.6 – AWS console showing Assign MFA device option

The next step is to prepare the AWS account for ROSA provisioning. This includes configuring an AWS account to satisfy the OpenShift prerequisites.

Preparing AWS for ROSA provisioning

To install ROSA services on AWS, we first need to enable the ROSA service. To enable ROSA, start by logging in as the `admin` user that you created in the previous stage and follow these steps:

1. Go to the AWS console and type `ROSA` in the services search bar. Click on the ROSA service, as shown in *Figure 2.7*:

Figure 2.7 – AWS service search showing ROSA

2.   Click on the **Get started** button on the ROSA page.

3.   You will see the page shown in *Figure 2.8*, which summarizes the ROSA prerequisites. ROSA is a managed service where Red Hat SREs, together with AWS engineers, manage the OpenShift cluster for you. Select the **I agree to share my contact information with Red Hat** checkbox and click on **Enable ROSA**:

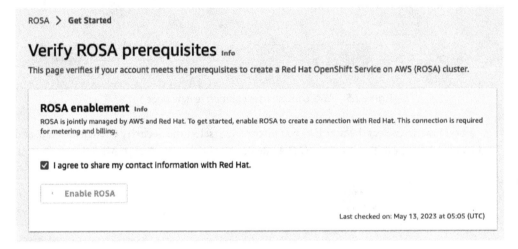

Figure 2.8 – ROSA prerequisites page

4.   On the same page, configure the service quota for ROSA. As you see in the next screenshot, the account I have created does not have the required service quota. Click on the **Increase service quotas** button if applicable to your cluster:

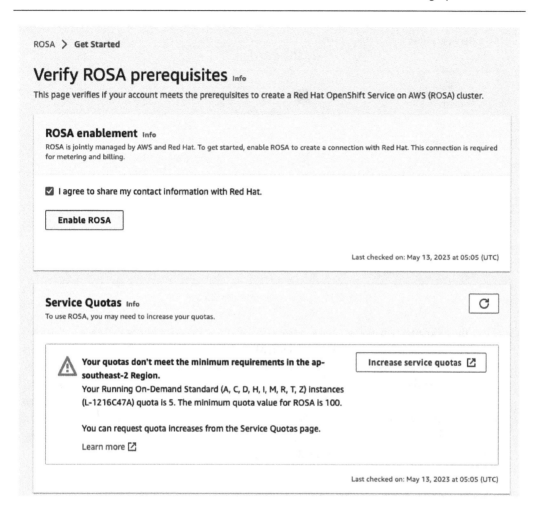

ROSA > **Get Started**

Verify ROSA prerequisites Info

This page verifies if your account meets the prerequisites to create a Red Hat OpenShift Service on AWS (ROSA) cluster.

ROSA enablement Info

ROSA is jointly managed by AWS and Red Hat. To get started, enable ROSA to create a connection with Red Hat. This connection is required for metering and billing.

☑ I agree to share my contact information with Red Hat.

    Enable ROSA

Last checked on: May 13, 2023 at 05:05 (UTC)

Service Quotas Info

To use ROSA, you may need to increase your quotas.

⚠ **Your quotas don't meet the minimum requirements in the ap-southeast-2 Region.**

Your Running On-Demand Standard (A, C, D, H, I, M, R, T, Z) instances (L-1216C47A) quota is 5. The minimum quota value for ROSA is 100.

You can request quota increases from the Service Quotas page.

Learn more ☑

    Increase service quotas ☑

Last checked on: May 13, 2023 at 05:05 (UTC)

Figure 2.9 – ROSA prerequisite page showing service quota requirements

5. You will be taken to the **Service Quotas** dashboard. Select the **Amazon Elastic Compute Cloud (Amazon EC2)** service, as shown in *Figure 2.10*:

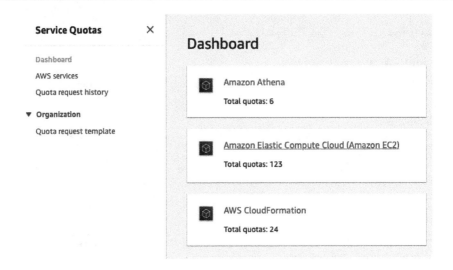

Figure 2.10 – Service Quotas dashboard

6.   Select the following two quotas, one at a time, and click on **Request quota increase** for each of them. The first one is **All Standard (A, C, H, I, M, R, T, Z) Spot Instance Requests**, as shown in *Figure 2.11*. This is to allow us to host some of the services on spot instances. These are cheaper alternatives to other computing resources. Remember that you do not need to choose this one, but we want to show you that with the OpenShift platform, you can run workloads, such as build pipelines, on spot instances to save costs. The second quota request is for on-demand instances, which you can find by searching for **L-1216C47A** in the console. This is for requesting standard **Elastic Compute Cloud (EC2)** instances to serve as OpenShift hosts:

Figure 2.11 – Service quota increase selection

7.   From the previous step, you will see the **Request quota increase** screen. Change the quota value in the **Change quota value** box to **256** for the spot instances and **100** for the on-demand instances. Click on the **Request** button:

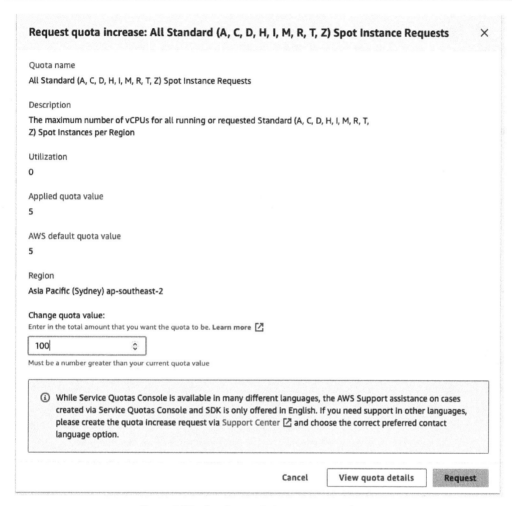

Figure 2.12 – Service quota increase request page

8. You can select **Quota request history** to see the status of your request. This usually takes a few minutes before it gets approved and closed.

9. After the service quota increase request is approved and the request closed, you should see a screen like the one shown in *Figure 2.13*. You will see that the last part of the prerequisite is about a role that ROSA uses to create AWS components for you. It should be automatically created since we give our `admin` users full rights:

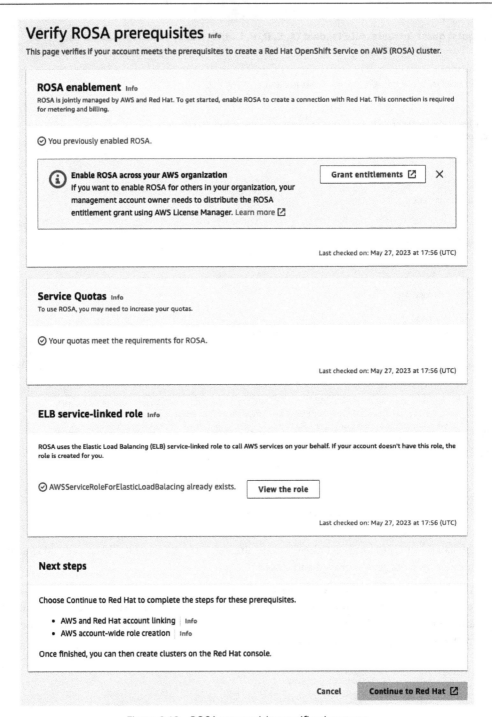

Figure 2.13 – ROSA prerequisites verification page

10. On the same page, when all of the prerequisite items are satisfied, click the **Continue to Red Hat** button on the last part of the page. A new page will be opened on the Red Hat site where you deploy a ROSA cluster.

This completes the second stage of the ROSA provisioning process where you have completed all the prerequisites required for installing the ROSA cluster. When you have been redirected to the Red Hat console website, and if you do not have an account with Red Hat, you can create an account at this stage. After you create the Red Hat account, you will be redirected to the Red Hat Hybrid Cloud Console, which is the last stage of the ROSA provisioning process.

> **Important Note**
>
> Note that for the account linking to work, make sure that the email that you used for the AWS account is the same email address for the Red Hat account.

Now that you have enabled the ROSA service on our AWS account and satisfied the ROSA prerequisites, the next step is to install the ROSA cluster.

Installing ROSA

In the Red Hat Hybrid Cloud Console, you will be presented with all the information required to create an OpenShift cluster on the AWS infrastructure. The ROSA installer will create all the AWS resources the cluster needs. The following steps will guide you through the installation of the OpenShift cluster:

1. The first page that you will be taken to after you finish the previous stage is the Red Hat Hybrid Cloud Console. This console allows you to manage all Red Hat cloud services, including ROSA.

   You may be required to accept the **Terms and Conditions** before you will see the cluster creation screen, like the one shown in *Figure 2.14*. Since you have already enabled ROSA in the previous section, you do not need to execute **Step 1** on this screen. For the second step, we will be using AWS CloudShell to execute the ROSA CLI command, so you can avoid this step too. The ROSA CLI is a command-line utility for managing ROSA instances.

   Download the ROSA CLI and follow the instructions on **Step 2** of the page, as shown in *Figure 2.14*. Depending on the operating system of your machine where you will be initiating the provisioning, the instructions may vary:

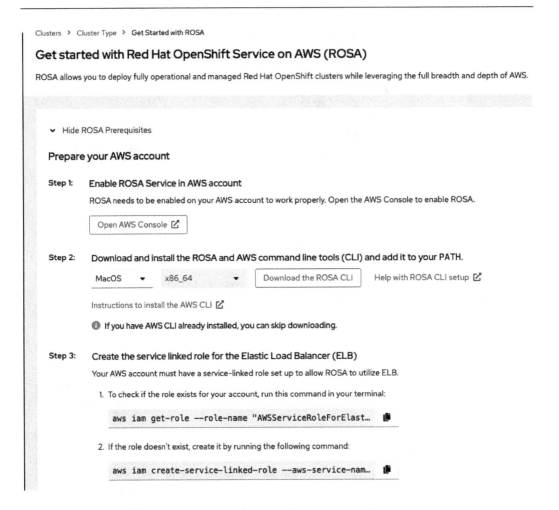

Figure 2.14 – Cluster creation page of the Red Hat Hybrid Cloud Console

2.   As shown in **Step 3** of the Red Hat console cluster creation page, verify that the right role is correctly assigned to the IAM user you are currently using. You can run these commands by opening your AWS console, in a new tab, and clicking on the "cloud shell" icon, as shown in *Figure 2.15*. The first command will tell you if the role exists. The second command may return an error if the role already exists, which you can safely ignore:

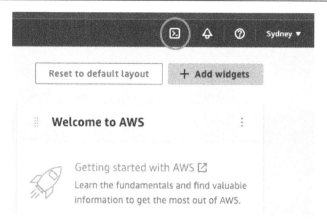

Figure 2.15 – AWS CloudShell launch icon

3.   Before you run the remaining steps from the **Get started on ROSA** screen, you will need to download and install the ROSA CLI into your CloudShell environment. Go to the cloud shell and run the following commands to download and install the ROSA client:

```
curl -O -L https://mirror.openshift.com/pub/openshift-v4/client/
rosa/latest/rosa-linux.tar.gz
tar -xvzf rosa-linux.tar
echo PATH=$PATH:/home/cloudshell-user >> ~/.bashrc
```

The ROSA CLI download path also varies depending on which operating system you will be running the CLI. The CloudShell environment is a Linux environment, which is why the given command in this example points to the Linux version of the ROSA CLI.

For a complete list of ROSA CLI binaries for all operating systems, go to `https://mirror.openshift.com/pub/openshift-v4/clients/rosa/latest/`.

> **Note**
> Please note that installing the AWS CLI on your local machine is optional if you are using CloudShell.

4.   Now, run the commands from **Step 4**. These commands will authenticate you against the ROSA service and create roles and policies that are needed for ROSA:

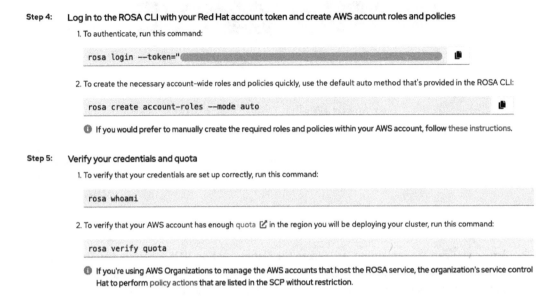

Step 4:   Log in to the ROSA CLI with your Red Hat account token and create AWS account roles and policies

  1. To authenticate, run this command:

```
rosa login --token="███████████████████████████████████████
```

  2. To create the necessary account-wide roles and policies quickly, use the default auto method that's provided in the ROSA CLI:

```
rosa create account-roles --mode auto
```

  ⓘ If you would prefer to manually create the required roles and policies within your AWS account, follow these instructions.

Step 5:   Verify your credentials and quota

  1. To verify that your credentials are set up correctly, run this command:

```
rosa whoami
```

  2. To verify that your AWS account has enough quota ⧉ in the region you will be deploying your cluster, run this command:

```
rosa verify quota
```

  ⓘ If you're using AWS Organizations to manage the AWS accounts that host the ROSA service, the organization's service control Hat to perform policy actions that are listed in the SCP without restriction.

Figure 2.16 – Red Hat console cluster creation page steps 4 and 5

You can see an output that says **AWS quota ok**.

5. Now, in the same cloud shell, create the ROSA cluster by running the following command. An interactive shell has been used to answer the configuration questions asked by the installer. You can get details of these options at https://docs.openshift.com/rosa/ rosa_install_access_delete_clusters/rosa_getting_started_iam/ rosa-creating-cluster.html. For this book, you can use the answers provided in *Table 2.1*. This is a long list of questions, and we have added our comments for each question to help guide you during this process:

```
rosa create cluster -sts
```

This command will initiate a prompt of questions that will configure the OpenShift installer and then begin the installation process.

For the region and availability zone options, we recommend that you choose the region and availability zone that is closest to your location. For more information about AWS regions and availability zones, see https://docs.aws.amazon.com/AmazonRDS/latest/ UserGuide/Concepts.RegionsAndAvailabilityZones.html.

The configuration provided here is aimed at provisioning a ROSA cluster for the purpose of performing the exercises in this book. This configuration should not be used for production clusters:

Prompt	Recommendation	Example
Cluster Name	Choose a cluster name	`mlops-test`
Deploy cluster with hosted control plane? (optional)	Choose N for less complexity. The Y options will require an **OpenID Connect (OIDC)** configuration upfront. Enabling this means that the control plane will be fully managed by Red Hat and that you will not have access to it. However, you will also not be billed by AWS for the control plane resources utilization. This option is similar to how AWS **Elastic Kubernetes Service (EKS)** is hosted.	N
OpenShift version	Choose the latest available version of OpenShift from the list. As of the writing of this book, we have tested the exercises in OpenShift version 4.13.0.	`4.13.0`
External ID (optional)	Leave this blank	
Operator roles prefix	Use the default	`mlops-test-b2p4`
Deploy cluster using pre-registered OIDC Configuration ID	Choose N for simplicity; you will be the only user of this cluster.	N
Tags	You can add any tags as necessary to identify this cluster if you have multiple ROSA clusters in your AWS account.	`rosa:mlops`
Multiple availability zones (optional)	Choose N for this cluster. Do not use N for production clusters.	N
AWS region	Choose N for this cluster. Do not use N for production clusters.	`ap-southeast-2`

Prompt	Recommendation	Example
Private link cluster (optional)	No. This is only required if you need to connect this cluster through a private link such as your on-premises data center.	N
Install into existing VPC (optional)	No. We want this cluster to be on its own **virtual private cloud (VPC)**.	N
Availability zone	Choose the zone closest to you	`ap-southeast-2a`
Enable Customer Managed key (optional)	Choose N for simplicity	N
Compute nodes instance type	Choose the recommended `m5.xlarge` type	`m5.xlarge`
Enable autoscaling (optional)	Choose N for simplicity. This means the cluster size will be fixed.	N
Compute nodes	Choose two worker nodes. You may choose more if you want. However, you must take note that this will incur more costs.	2
Default machine pool labels (optional)	Leave this blank as we are not using them for the exercises	
Machine CIDR	Use default	`10.0.0.0/16`
Service CIDR	Use default	`172.30.0.0/16`
Pod CIDR	Use default	`10.128.0.0/14`
Host prefix	Use default	`23`
Enable FIPS support (optional)	No. **Federal Information Processing Standards (FIPS)** are required only by the US federal government.	N
Encrypt `etcd` data (optional)	No	N
Disable Workload monitoring (optional)	No. You should only disable this if you plan to implement your own workload monitoring.	N

Table 2.1 – OpenShift installer configuration

After answering the last question, this will create the ROSA resource in your AWS account.

6. Check the status of the cluster you have just created by running the following command:

    ```
    rosa list clusters
    rosa describe cluster -c mlops-test
    ```

7. The first command will list all the ROSA clusters in your AWS account or organization, including the one you have just created. You will see that the status is set to **Waiting**. The second command will display details of the cluster. In the cluster details, you should see the status as **Waiting (Waiting for OIDC Configuration)**. OIDC is the IAM protocol that will be used in your cluster.

8. Run the following commands to create and configure the default OIDC provider in AWS:

    ```
    rosa create operator-roles --cluster mlops-test
    rosa create oidc-provider --cluster mlops-test
    ```

9. Once the OIDC provider is created, it should initiate the OpenShift installation process. The installation process will take up to 30 minutes or more, so get ready to grab a tea or coffee while waiting for the process to complete.

    The installer will provision **virtual machines** (**VMs**) on AWS, create load balancers, and install and set up OpenShift on those machines, among many other things, before it completes.

10. Meanwhile, you can check on the progress of the installation in the Red Hat Hybrid Cloud Console. Open `http://console.redhat.com/openshift` in a new tab to start managing your cluster.

11. Select the **Clusters** menu item from the left-hand side of the page, and you will see the status of your OpenShift cluster as **Installing cluster**. Click on the cluster name to see details of the installation progress, as shown in *Figure 2.17*:

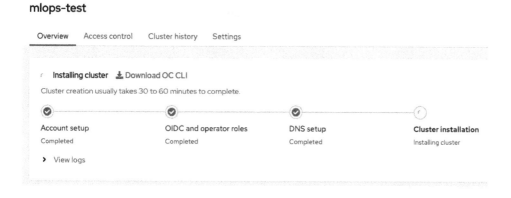

Figure 2.17 – Red Hat Hybrid Cloud Console showing the installation progress

12. Once the cluster has been provisioned and is ready for use, you will see a **Ready** status of the cluster on the same screen, as shown in *Figure 2.18*:

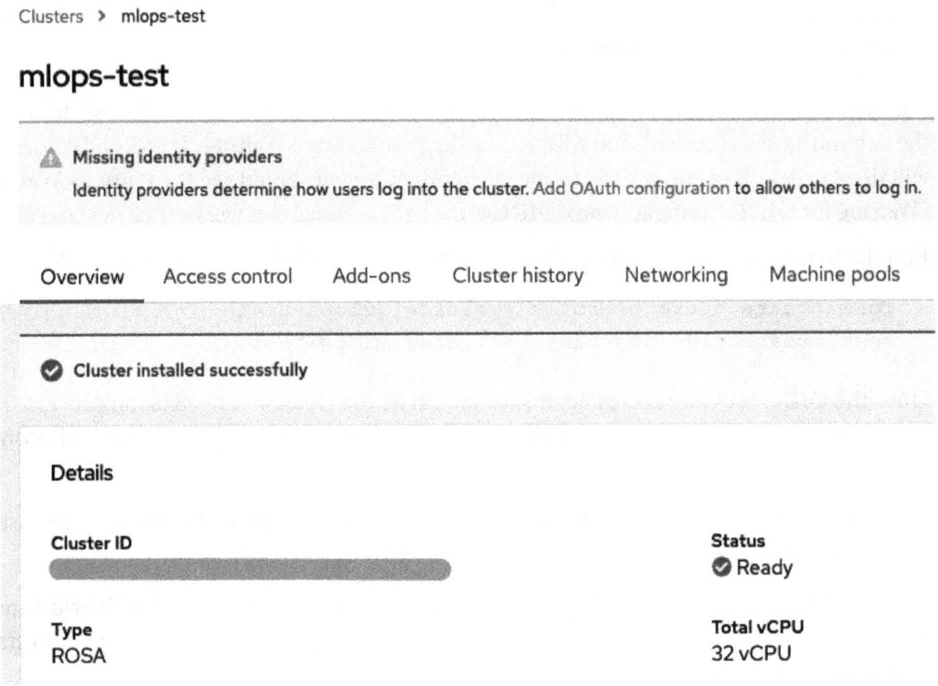

Clusters > mlops-test

mlops-test

⚠ **Missing identity providers**
  Identity providers determine how users log into the cluster. Add OAuth configuration to allow others to log in.

Overview   Access control   Add-ons   Cluster history   Networking   Machine pools

✅ **Cluster installed successfully**

Details

Cluster ID
▬▬▬▬▬▬▬▬▬▬▬▬▬▬

Type
ROSA

Status
✅ Ready

Total vCPU
32 vCPU

Figure 2.18 – Red Hat Hybrid Cloud Console showing the completed installation

13. The next stage is to create a new user for your cluster. This can be managed from the **Access control** tab of the OpenShift page of the Red Hat Hybrid Cloud Console. OpenShift can integrate with several **Open Authorization 2 (OAuth 2)** and OIDC IdPs, including your corporate **Lightweight Directory Access Protocol (LDAP)** directory. You can also add more than one IdP to a cluster:

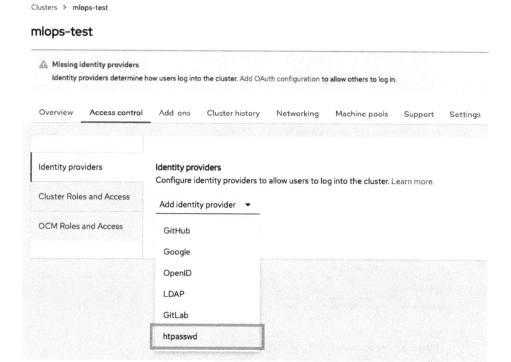

Figure 2.19 – Access control page showing a list of IdPs

For simplicity, we will use a basic **htpasswd** provider.

14. Select the **htpasswd** option, and you will be presented with a screen to create a username and password pair, as shown in *Figure 2.20*. In the user screen for the **htpasswd** provider, set the username as `mlops-admin` and put in the password that you want. This user and password will be used to access the OpenShift cluster and provision the MLOps components. Click on the **Add** button after you enter your custom password:

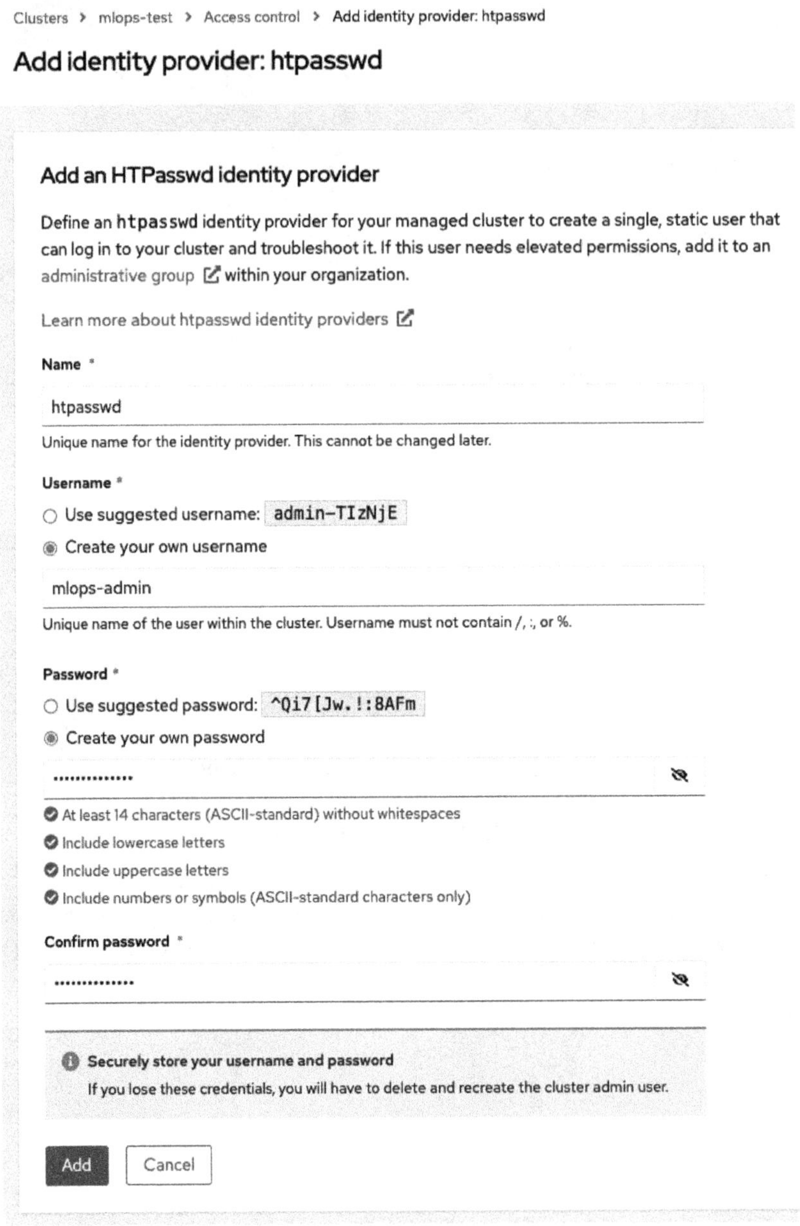

Clusters > mlops-test > Access control > Add identity provider: htpasswd

Add identity provider: htpasswd

Add an HTPasswd identity provider

Define an htpasswd identity provider for your managed cluster to create a single, static user that can log in to your cluster and troubleshoot it. If this user needs elevated permissions, add it to an administrative group ☑ within your organization.

Learn more about htpasswd identity providers ☑

Name *

    htpasswd

Unique name for the identity provider. This cannot be changed later.

Username *

○ Use suggested username: `admin-TIzNjE`

◉ Create your own username

    mlops-admin

Unique name of the user within the cluster. Username must not contain /, :, or %.

Password *

○ Use suggested password: `^Qi7[Jw.!:8AFm`

◉ Create your own password

    ••••••••••••••   👁‍🗨

✔ At least 14 characters (ASCII-standard) without whitespaces
✔ Include lowercase letters
✔ Include uppercase letters
✔ Include numbers or symbols (ASCII-standard characters only)

Confirm password *

    ••••••••••••••   👁‍🗨

ⓘ **Securely store your username and password**
   If you lose these credentials, you will have to delete and recreate the cluster admin user.

[Add]   [Cancel]

Figure 2.20 – htpassword configuration screen

15. The next stage is to assign a cluster administrator role to the `mlops-admin` user that you have just created. Go to the **Access control** tab, select the **Cluster Roles and Access** option, and click on the **Add user** button:

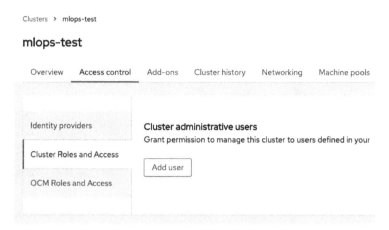

Figure 2.21 – Cluster roles page

16. Give the `mlops-admin` user the role of `cluster-admin`. This is a full-access role for your OpenShift cluster. We would like to reiterate that for production clusters, you will have more stricter controls. The aim of the book is not to learn how to manage OpenShift but to provide you with enough details so that you can start building your own MLOps system. The screen shown in *Figure 2.22* shows how you will associate the `cluster-admin` role with the `mlops-admin` user. Hit the **Add user** button under the **cluster-admins** user role:

Figure 2.22 – Add cluster user dialog

17. Your cluster is ready to be logged in to. In the top-right corner of the Red Hat console, there is a button that takes you to the OpenShift web console. Click the button, as shown in *Figure 2.23*.

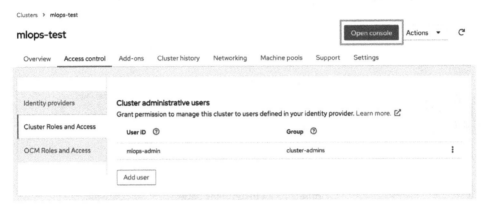

Figure 2.23 – Cluster page showing the Open console button

18. You will be presented with the OpenShift login button, as shown next, with the authentication provider that you have chosen. Click on **htpasswd** and enter the credentials for the mlops-admin user that you have created:

Figure 2.24 – OpenShift web console login screen

The login options will become a list of IdPs if you add multiple IdPs to your cluster.

19. The TLS certificate may not be valid immediately after installation. The cluster takes a few minutes to update the TLS certificate. If you log in before the certificates are created, you may encounter a certificate error. You can bypass the certificate errors at this point. After a successful login, you will be taken to the OpenShift web console landing page, as shown in *Figure 2.25*:

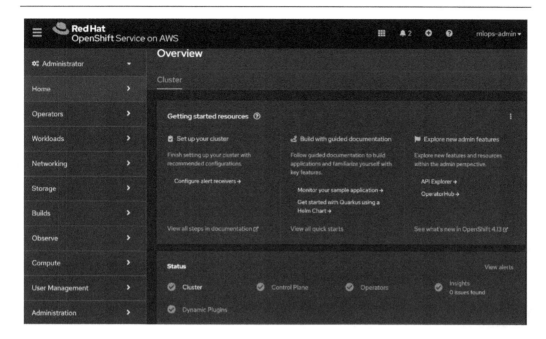

Figure 2.25 – OpenShift web console

Voilà! You have just provisioned a new Red Hat OpenShift cluster on AWS that will become the base for your new MLOps platform.

Now that you have a running OpenShift cluster on AWS, let's have a look at options for customizing the compute resources of your cluster.

Adding a new machine pool to the cluster

Adding a machine pool is an optional step that you can do if you want to have additional control over what kinds of machines will be created and added to your OpenShift cluster. This is usually done if you have heterogeneous host machines or if you have specific hardware units in some of your worker nodes and you want to tag these nodes from the rest of the regular worker nodes. This is OpenShift's way of provisioning groups of worker nodes by capability. This is useful when running ML model training workloads on demand as you may require worker nodes that have special *compute* units in them. You may use this approach to create machines that have **graphics processing units** (**GPUs**) or other hardware resources that are vital in model training.

You may add extra machines or worker nodes to host specific workloads. You can manage them from the Red Hat Hybrid Cloud Console through the following steps:

1. Select your `mlops-test` cluster, and then click on the **Machine pools** tab and click **Add machine pool**.

2. You will be presented with the following screen. You can select spot instances or general on-demand instances, as shown next. Spot instances provide up to 90% cost savings as compared to on-demand instances and may be a good choice for your learning cluster. It's your choice:

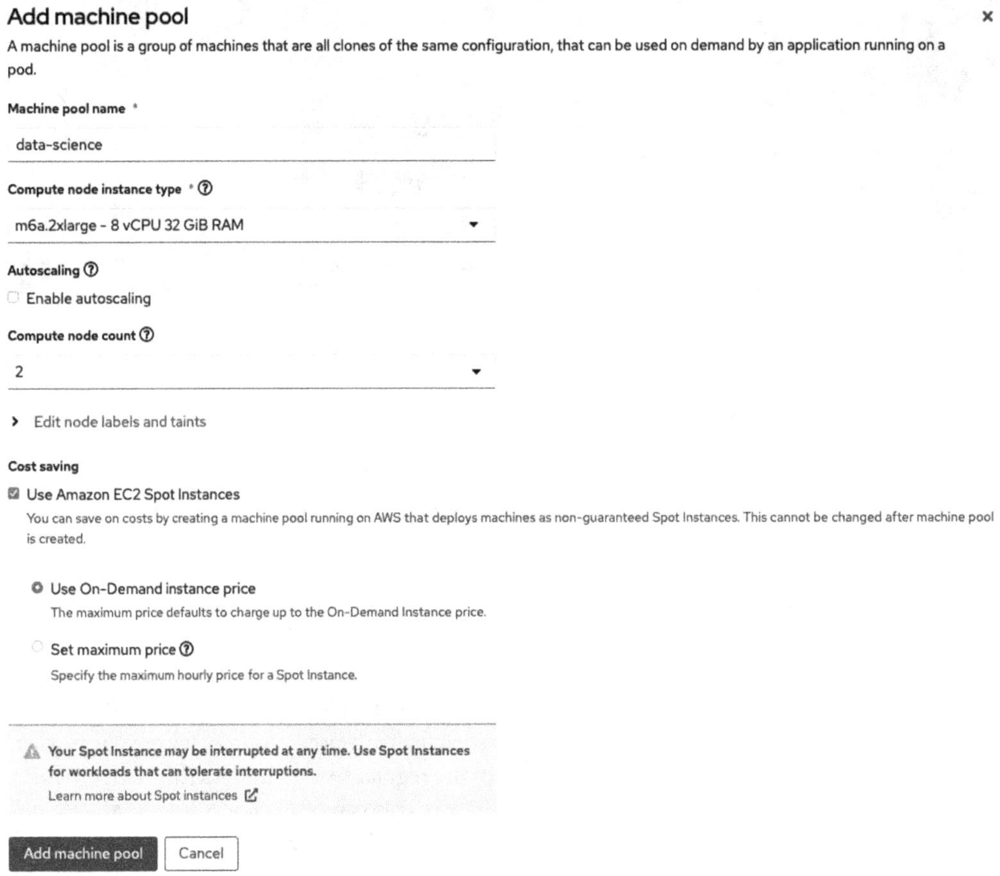

Add machine pool   ✕

A machine pool is a group of machines that are all clones of the same configuration, that can be used on demand by an application running on a pod.

Machine pool name *

    data-science

Compute node instance type * ⑦

    m6a.2xlarge - 8 vCPU 32 GiB RAM   ▾

Autoscaling ⑦

    ☐ Enable autoscaling

Compute node count ⑦

    2   ▾

> Edit node labels and taints

Cost saving

☑ Use Amazon EC2 Spot Instances

   You can save on costs by creating a machine pool running on AWS that deploys machines as non-guaranteed Spot Instances. This cannot be changed after machine pool is created.

   ◉ Use On-Demand instance price
      The maximum price defaults to charge up to the On-Demand Instance price.

   ○ Set maximum price ⑦
      Specify the maximum hourly price for a Spot Instance.

   ⚠ **Your Spot Instance may be interrupted at any time. Use Spot Instances for workloads that can tolerate interruptions.**
      Learn more about Spot instances ☑

[Add machine pool]   [Cancel]

Figure 2.26 – OpenShift page for adding machine pools

3. Click on the **Add machine pool** button if you want to add more machines. You can choose to add them later as you progress in the book. After that, go back to your OpenShift console and select **Compute** -> **MachineSets** from the left-hand menu to validate that the machines are available to the cluster:

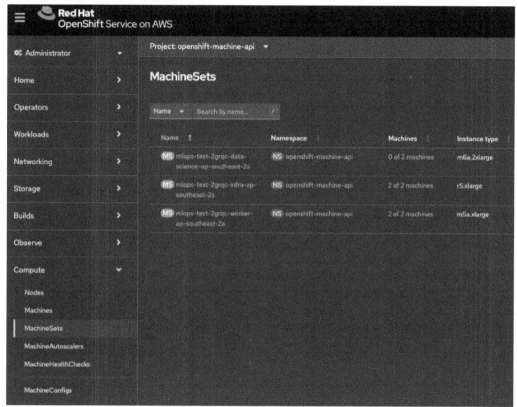

Figure 2.27 – MachineSets screen

We have come a long way. Now, our OpenShift cluster is ready for business. You have seen how the cloud and OpenShift made it easy for you to provision a fully functional managed platform, such as OpenShift. This cloud capability allows you to focus on delivering business value instead of configuring infrastructure.

The process of installing ROSA has provisioned the following major infrastructure components in AWS for you:

- Three units of `m5.2xlarge` EC2 instances as control-plane nodes

- Two units of `r5.xlarge` EC2 instances as infrastructure nodes

- Two units of `m5.xlarge` EC2 instances as customizable worker nodes

- Storage resources for all the nodes with 350 GB storage capacity for the control-plane nodes and 300 GB for the other nodes

- Load balancers for OpenShift API and an ingress controller for the applications

- An internal image registry backed by **Simple Storage Service** (**S3**) object storage

The installer also installed the Red Hat Linux operating system on the EC2 machines and installed the required OpenShift software for you to use. Neat!

Now you have the cluster, the next stage is to install Red Hat ODS on the OpenShift cluster.

Installing Red Hat ODS

The Red Hat ODS service enables data science teams to execute data science and ML workflows by integrating Red Hat components, **open source software** (**OSS**), and partner offerings. Its primary goal is to provide a collaborative and scalable environment for data scientists and data engineers to develop, deploy, and manage ML and AI applications.

With ODS, data scientists can leverage familiar tools such as Jupyter Notebook to create interactive development environments for their data analysis and model development tasks. You can easily build and train ML models using frameworks such as TensorFlow, PyTorch, and scikit-learn. Red Hat ODS includes JupyterHub, Git integration, model deployment, and model serving and is based on the upstream open source project, **Open Data Hub** (**ODH**). You will learn more about the details and internal components of Red Hat ODS in the next chapters.

OpenShift makes it very easy to install ODS in the following easy steps. ODS is packaged as a Kubernetes operator available in OperatorHub (`https://operatorhub.io`). OperatorHub comes with every OpenShift cluster and is embedded as part of the OpenShift web console. This allows cluster administrators to discover and install Kubernetes operators without leaving the OpenShift web console.

The following steps will guide you through the process of installing an ODS operator onto our cluster. The installation steps also apply to other flavors of OpenShift, regardless of the infrastructure it is running on:

1. Log in to your OpenShift console and navigate to the **Operators** -> **OperatorHub** option in the left-hand menu. Then, on the right-hand side panel, search for **Red Hat OpenShift Data Science**. The list should show one item called **Red Hat OpenShift Data Science**. Select this item, as shown in *Figure 2.28*:

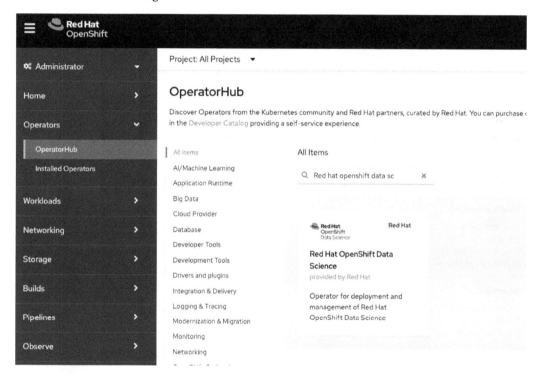

Figure 2.28 – OperatorHub showing Red Hat OpenShift Data Science operator

2. Click on the **Red Hat OpenShift Data Science** tile, and you will be presented with a details screen, as shown in *Figure 2.29*. Click the **Install** button on this screen to install the operator:

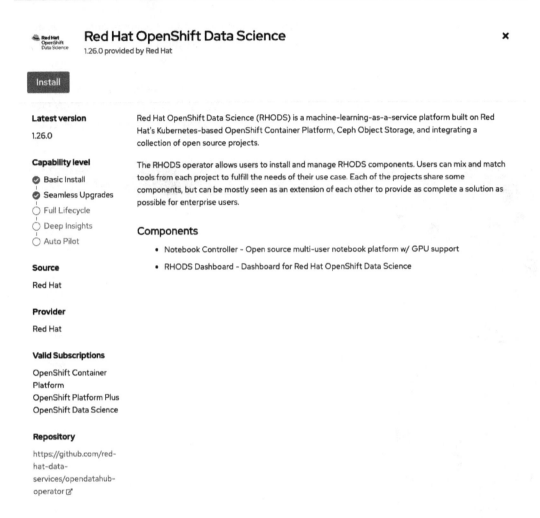

Figure 2.29 – ODS operator details screen

3.   After clicking the **Install** button, you will be presented with an installation configuration screen.
     Use the default settings. The **All namespaces on the cluster** installation mode makes the operator
     available to all users and namespaces in the cluster. When you choose the automatic updates
     option for **Update approval**, this operator will be automatically upgraded by the **Operator
     Lifecycle Manager** (**OLM**) whenever a new version of that Operator is available in the selected
     update channel. Some teams choose to select manual approval to add a level of control as to
     when to upgrade the operator. You may also want to set the update approval option to **Manual**
     for production environments. Operator upgrades sometimes deprecate certain APIs and may
     cause disruptions to existing resources managed by the operator.

Click on the **Install** button on the screen shown in *Figure 2.30* to start the installation of the Red Hat ODS operator. This will take you to the operator installation progress screen:

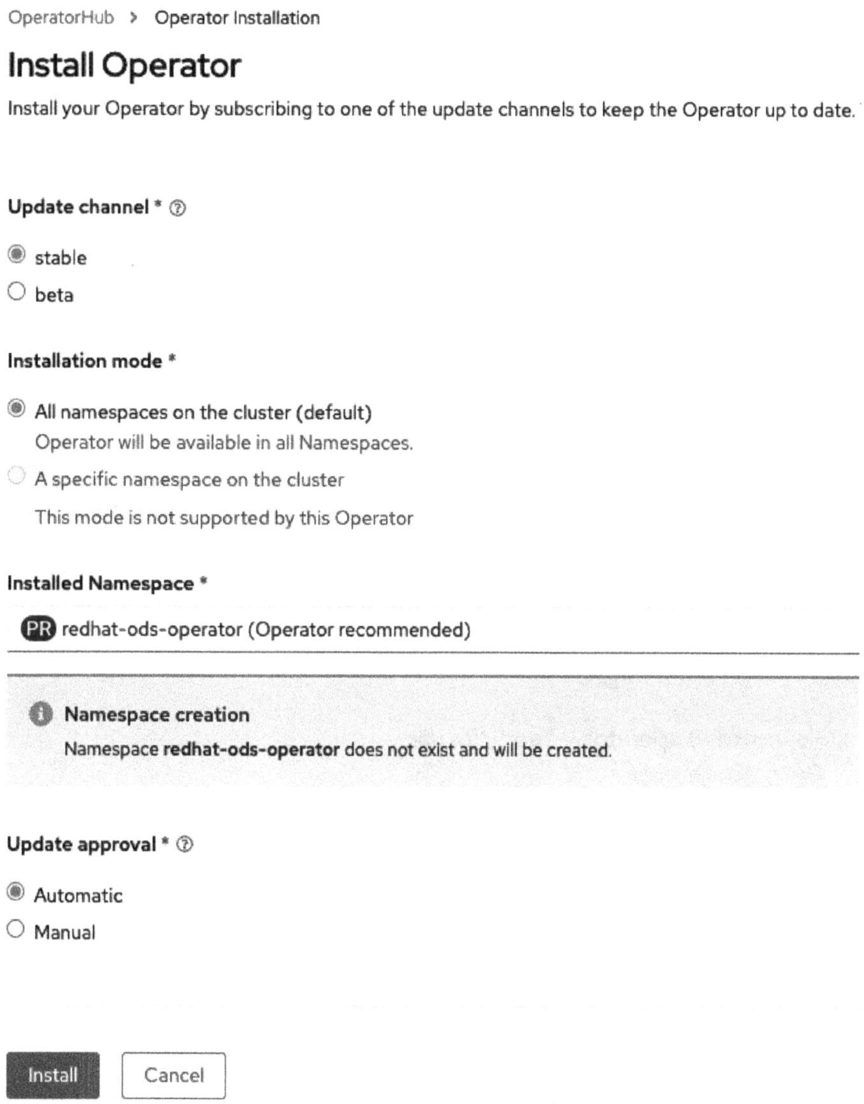

OperatorHub > Operator Installation

Install Operator

Install your Operator by subscribing to one of the update channels to keep the Operator up to date.

Update channel * ⑦

◉ stable

○ beta

Installation mode *

◉ All namespaces on the cluster (default)
   Operator will be available in all Namespaces.

○ A specific namespace on the cluster

   This mode is not supported by this Operator

Installed Namespace *

PR redhat-ods-operator (Operator recommended)

ⓘ **Namespace creation**
   Namespace **redhat-ods-operator** does not exist and will be created.

Update approval * ⑦

◉ Automatic

○ Manual

[Install]   [Cancel]

Figure 2.30 – Operator installation options

4. Wait for the operator installation progress to complete. The operator installation progress will show progress as **Installing Operator**, as shown in *Figure 2.31*:

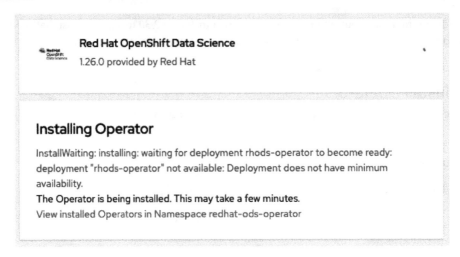

Figure 2.31 – Operator installation progress dialog

After the installation is complete, you should see a screen similar to the one shown in *Figure 2.32*, showing the **View Operator** button:

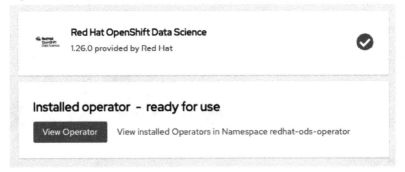

Figure 2.32 – Operator installation dialog showing a successful install

The operator installation process will have created multiple namespaces for you, and they are described as follows:

- The `redhat-ods-operator` namespace contains the ODS operator.

- The `redhat-ods-applications` namespace installs the dashboard and other required components of ODS.

- The `redhat-ods-monitoring` project contains services for monitoring. It uses Prometheus as the monitoring stack.

- The `rhods-notebooks` project is where default notebook environments are deployed.

- This operator installation also added a new shortcut menu item in the web console to navigate to the ODS dashboard. You may access the ODS console as shown in *Figure 2.33*:

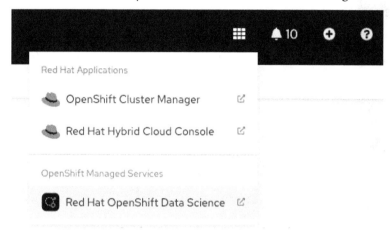

Figure 2.33 – ODS shortcut from a web console

And that's it. How easy is it to deploy ODS? Now, your ODS installation is complete. Let's install partner and open source components in the next section.

Installing partner software on RedHat ODS

In order to complete our MLOps platform, we will need to install additional tools to OpenShift to complement the features of ODS. Several tools are considered partner software of the ODS platform. These software products are listed in the ODS console and can be viewed by clicking the **Explore** menu item in the ODS console, as shown in *Figure 2.34*:

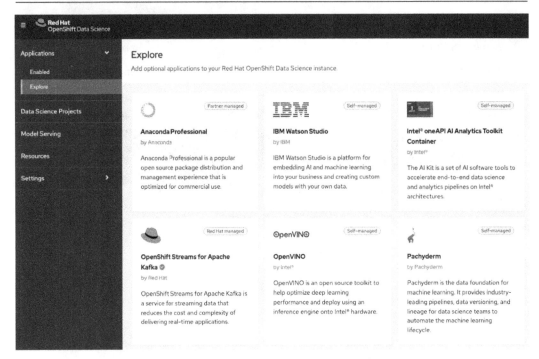

Figure 2.34 – ODS console showing partner software

One of the things that you will need to complete the MLOps platform is data versioning, and you will need data lineage too. We will use **Pachyderm** for this need.

Pachyderm is a powerful OSS tool designed to manage data in modern data pipelines. It serves as a data versioning and lineage system, enabling efficient tracking and control of data changes throughout the data processing life cycle.

With Pachyderm, you can easily keep track of modifications made to your data, similar to how **version control systems (VCS)** such as Git track changes in code. This ensures that you have a clear understanding of how your data evolves over time, allowing you to compare different versions effortlessly.

One of the key strengths of Pachyderm lies in its ability to build scalable and reproducible data pipelines. By defining a series of processing steps using containers, Pachyderm automates the execution of these steps on your data. It takes care of parallelization, managing dependencies, and ensuring **fault tolerance (FT)**, allowing you to focus on the analysis rather than the infrastructure.

Similar to a VCS for code, Pachyderm serves as a data VCS. It offers a familiar Git-like interface, enabling cloning, branching, merging, and forking of data repositories. This facilitates collaboration among data scientists and analysts, as they can work on the same dataset, experiment with different approaches, and keep track of changes.

Pachyderm is built to handle large-scale data processing and provides scalability and parallelization capabilities. It efficiently distributes data and processing across a cluster of machines, ensuring optimal performance. Parallel execution of tasks is also supported, which is particularly beneficial when dealing with extensive datasets.

Overall, Pachyderm simplifies the management of data in complex projects. It ensures reproducibility, fosters collaboration, and provides traceability in data science, ML, and analytics workflows, where data is always evolving.

Now, let's take a look at how to install Pachyderm into your OpenShift cluster.

Installing Pachyderm

Because Pachyderm is a Kubernetes-native platform, it can also natively run on OpenShift. Pachyderm is available as a Kubernetes operator in OperatorHub.

The following steps will guide you through the operator installation of Pachyderm:

1. In the OpenShift console, navigate to **Operators** -> **OperatorHub**.

2. Search for **Pachyderm**. You should see Pachyderm shown as a tile, as shown in *Figure 2.35*:

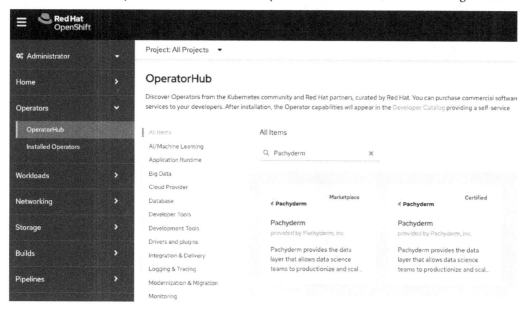

Figure 2.35 – OperatorHub showing Pachyderm

3. If you are presented with two options, as shown in *Figure 2.35*, choose the one tagged as **Certified** and then click the **Install** button. Certified operators are operators that are verified by Red Hat to run in OpenShift.

4. Use the default options in the **Install Operator** screen, as shown in *Figure 2.36*, and then click **Install**:

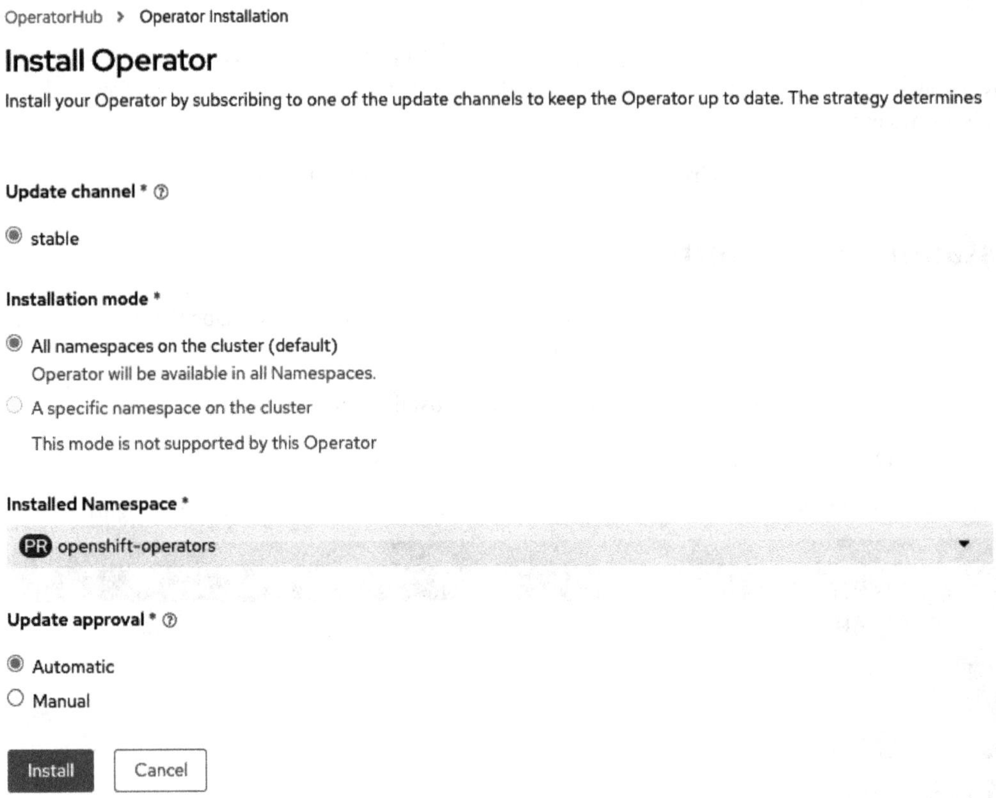

OperatorHub > Operator Installation

Install Operator

Install your Operator by subscribing to one of the update channels to keep the Operator up to date. The strategy determines

Update channel * ⑦

◉ stable

Installation mode *

◉ All namespaces on the cluster (default)
    Operator will be available in all Namespaces.

○ A specific namespace on the cluster
    This mode is not supported by this Operator

Installed Namespace *

PR openshift-operators   ▼

Update approval * ⑦

◉ Automatic
○ Manual

Install   Cancel

Figure 2.36 – Install Operator dialog of Pachyderm

5. Once the installation is complete, Pachyderm should be listed in your ODS portal's enabled applications, as shown in *Figure 2.37*:

Figure 2.37 – ODS console showing Pachyderm

The Pachyderm operator itself is not the Pachyderm instance. Instead, it manages instances of Pachyderm within your cluster.

Voilà! You have just installed the Pachyderm operator into your OpenShift cluster.

Summary

In this chapter, you have learned how to provision the platform. You have installed the Red Hat OpenShift platform, Red Hat ODS, and Pachyderm. You have seen how the MLOps components defined in the previous chapters are translated into the software components presented in this chapter. It gives you a mental model of what a complete MLOps platform would look like.

In the next few chapters, you will dive deeper into each of these components and understand how they enable your team to move forward. Now that you have learned how to install Kubernetes operators from OperatorHub. We will also be adding more open source components to your MLOps technology stack as you go through the later chapters.

3

Building Machine Learning Models with OpenShift

In the previous chapter, you installed and configured OpenShift to power your **machine learning (ML)** project life cycle. In this chapter, you will configure the platform components required for model development. This chapter will equip you with what is available on the OpenShift platform for building ML models and how your team can leverage it. Please ensure that you have completed the setup mentioned in the previous chapter before starting this chapter.

This is the first stage of the ML development life cycle, which we presented in *Chapter 2*. In this chapter, you will see how easy it is for you and your team to start building with the technology provided by **Red Hat OpenShift for Data Science (RHODS)**.

We will cover the following topics:

- Using Jupyter Notebooks in OpenShift
- Using ML frameworks in OpenShift
- Using GPU acceleration for model training
- Building custom notebooks

Technical requirements

In this chapter, you'll need to use this book's GitHub repository. This can be found at `https://github.com/PacktPublishing/MLOps-with-Red-Hat-OpenShift`. The files that you will need in this chapter are located in the `chapter3` directory. You will also write basic Python code to validate the deployments and configurations.

Using Jupyter Notebooks in OpenShift

Jupyter Notebooks is the de facto standard environment for data scientists and data engineers to analyze data and build ML models. Since the notebooks provided by the platform run as containers, you will see how your team can start quickly and consistently by adopting the platform. The platform provides a rapid way to develop, train, and test ML models and deploy them onto production. In the ODS platform, the Jupyter Notebooks environments are referred to as **workbenches**. You will learn about workbenches later in this section. But first, we need to learn how to create these environments.

We'll start by provisioning S3 object storage for you to access the data required for the model training process. This is part of the platform setup, and data scientists will not have to execute these steps for their day-to-day work.

Provisioning an S3 store

ML loves data. A lot of data! S3-compatible object storage software is becoming the de facto standard for storing and retrieving unstructured data at scale and is available on all three big cloud vendors. You can leverage Kubernetes-native open source tools such as **MinIO** to provision an S3-compatible object store on your OpenShift cluster. **MinIO** is a high-performance, S3-compatible object store that can be deployed on OpenShift, through which you can use it on-premises and in the cloud.

Red Hat also provides an integrated storage component on the OpenShift platform, named Open Data Foundation, that provides an S3-compatible API. Any standard S3-compatible object storage product will work with ODS. For this book, we've chosen MinIO for simplicity. So, let's start by installing MinIO on the OpenShift platform.

From the code repository for this book, go to the `chapter3` folder and find the `minio-complete.yaml` file. The following steps show how to use the `minio-complete.yaml` file to deploy the latest MinIO container onto the provisioned OpenShift cluster from the previous chapter. The YAML file contains the OpenShift Deployment, Pod, and Service definition for running MinIO. The file also creates a `PersistentVolumeClaim` request to be used by the MinIO Pod to store files. For this example, we'll be using a capacity of 10 Gi; you can change this in the YAML file if required. The username and password for MinIO are also configured in the file under the environment variables for the MinIO container. The file also creates an OpenShift route so that you can use the MinIO UI, as explained later in this chapter. We encourage you to familiarize yourself with the YAML file's content to get a better understanding of what is required to run a simple MinIO server in OpenShift:

1. Open the OpenShift console and create a new project named `ml-workshop`.

2. Click on the + icon on the top-right corner of the OpenShift console; you will see the following screen. Paste the `minio-complete.yaml` file into the **Import YAML** screen and hit the **Create** button:

Figure 3.1 – Importing the minio-complete.yaml file

3. Verify that the MinIO Pods are in a running state; you can check from the **Pods** view from the left menu in OpenShift. Once you have verified that MinIO has deployed, go to the **Routes** menu option under the **Networking** menu and find the route that has been created. This route can be seen in the following screenshot:

Figure 3.2 – MinIO OpenShift route

4.   Click on the route; you will be taken to the MinIO login console. Use a user ID of `minio` and a password of `minio123` to log in.

Congratulations! You have just installed the MinIO component on the Red Hat OpenShift platform. This is all you need to provision for MinIO for your teams to use it. You may choose to have multiple MinIO servers for different teams, but it depends on the strategy you implement for your specific use case.

Now, the data scientists can log in and start creating buckets to store and use the data for their ML development workflows. Let's see how the data scientists can use MinIO to create a bucket:

1.   After logging into the MinIO console, click on the **Buckets** menu option on the left-hand side; you will be presented with the following screen. Click on the **Create a Bucket** link:

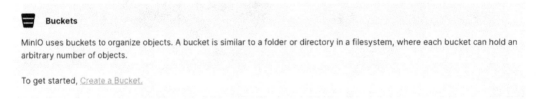

Figure 3.3 – The MinIO bucket console

2.   On the **Create Bucket** screen, name the bucket `demo-files` and click on the **Create Bucket** button:

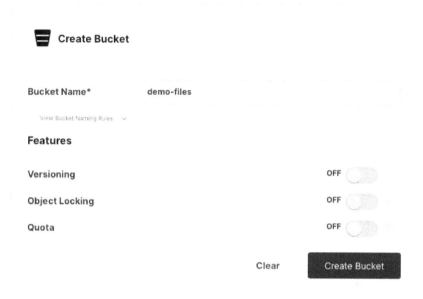

Figure 3.4 – MinIO's Create Bucket console

3. You will see that the bucket has been created. This is the bucket you will be using to store files for the rest of this chapter:

Figure 3.5 – Minio's "demo-files" bucket

Once the bucket has been created by the data scientists, they will start model building process using the Red Hat platform. In the OpenShift console, go to the **redhat-ods-application** project and click on the **Routes** link presented under the **Networking** menu option. Click on the route to go to the RHODS UI. You can see the route link in the following screenshot:

Figure 3.6 – RHODS route URL

You can start using RHODS by defining a new data science project. A project is a way to group different configurations data scientists need during the model development life cycle. For example, let's say that you are building a fraud detection model for personal credit cards; you would create a project called `fraud-detection-personal-credit-cards`. A project can have the following components:

- **Workbenches**: These are development environments within your project where you can access notebooks and generate models. You can have multiple workbenches in a project, such as one workbench for a model based on deep learning and another for a model based on *XGBoost*. You can compartmentalize your projects via workbenches in any way you want.

- **Cluster storage**: These provide storage for your project in your OpenShift cluster. This storage will be used by your notebooks; think of it as a disk associated with your development environment. You clone your repositories here and because the disk is provisioned by OpenShift, it could be backed up depending on the cluster policies.

- **Data connections**: A list of data sources that your project uses. This is where your training data, your temporary data, and others are stored. This is storage based on the S3 API. You can use **Red Hat Open Data Foundation** (**RHODF**) or other open source components, such as MinIO. You will be using the MinIO server you provisioned earlier in this chapter. You can also use native cloud storage; you do not have to use OpenShift-based storage. For on-premises installations, MinIO on OpenShift will provide S3-compatible object storage for you.

- **Models and model servers**: A list of models and model servers that your project uses. We will look at the model server in more detail later in this book. For now, consider it a component that can take your model and expose it as a service for consumption.

Let's create a new RHODS project by following these steps:

1. Once you've logged into the RHODS console, you will be presented with the following screen. Click on **Create data science project**:

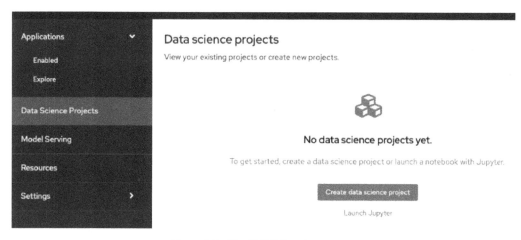

Figure 3.7 – The RHODS project screen

2. On the **Create data science project** screen, shown here, add the name and resource name as demo-project. The resource name will be used as an HTTP link for your development environment. Click on the **Create** button:

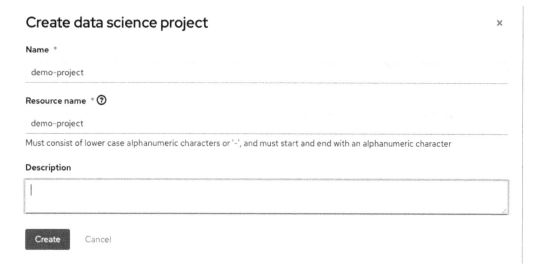

Figure 3.8 – RHODS – Create data science project

3. In **demo-project**, which you have just created, click on the **Create workbench** button:

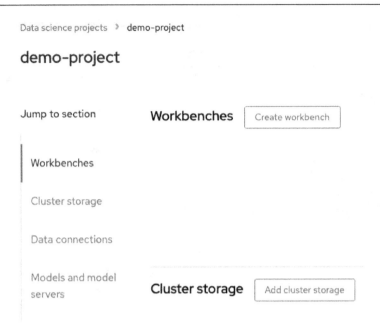

Figure 3.9 – RHODS – demo-project

4. Enter the name of the workbench as demo-workbench. You will see that the **Notebook image** section provides you with a list of container images. Red Hat provides prebuilt images for common libraries such as TensorFlow and PyTorch. Your team does not need to worry about packaging compatible libraries by utilizing the images provided by Red Hat. It will speed up your model development process and provide a consistent runtime environment for your teams. For this example, select the **Standard Data Science** image from the drop-down menu.

Data science projects > demo-project > Create workbench

Create workbench

Configure properties for your workbench.

Jump to section	
	Name *
	demo-workbench
Name and description	**Description**
Notebook image	
Deployment size	
Environment variables	**Notebook image**
	Image selection *
Cluster storage	Standard Data Science ▼
Data connections	**Version selection** *
	2023.1 (Recommended) ▼
	Hover an option to learn more information about the package.
	❷ View package information
	Deployment size
	Container size
	Small ▼

Figure 3.10 – RHODS – Create workbench

5.   The next option is **Deployment size**, where you allocate resources for your work. When you select the Container size drop-down menu, the platform will give you options for memory and CPU; select the amount you need. This is a fantastic way to share resources across team members as the team is using whatever is required. Later in this chapter, you will provision GPUs, after which the GPUs will be presented on this screen as a dropdown. In the Cluster storage section, which is the second part of the following screenshot, select the size of the disk you would like for your development needs. We start with 40 GB. You will see how RHODS makes it easier to share and use resources, which helps your team be more agile. Here, you can define the hardware and software requirements for your environment, after which the platform orchestrates all the requirements and gives you a fully functional environment within minutes. You can see all the options here:

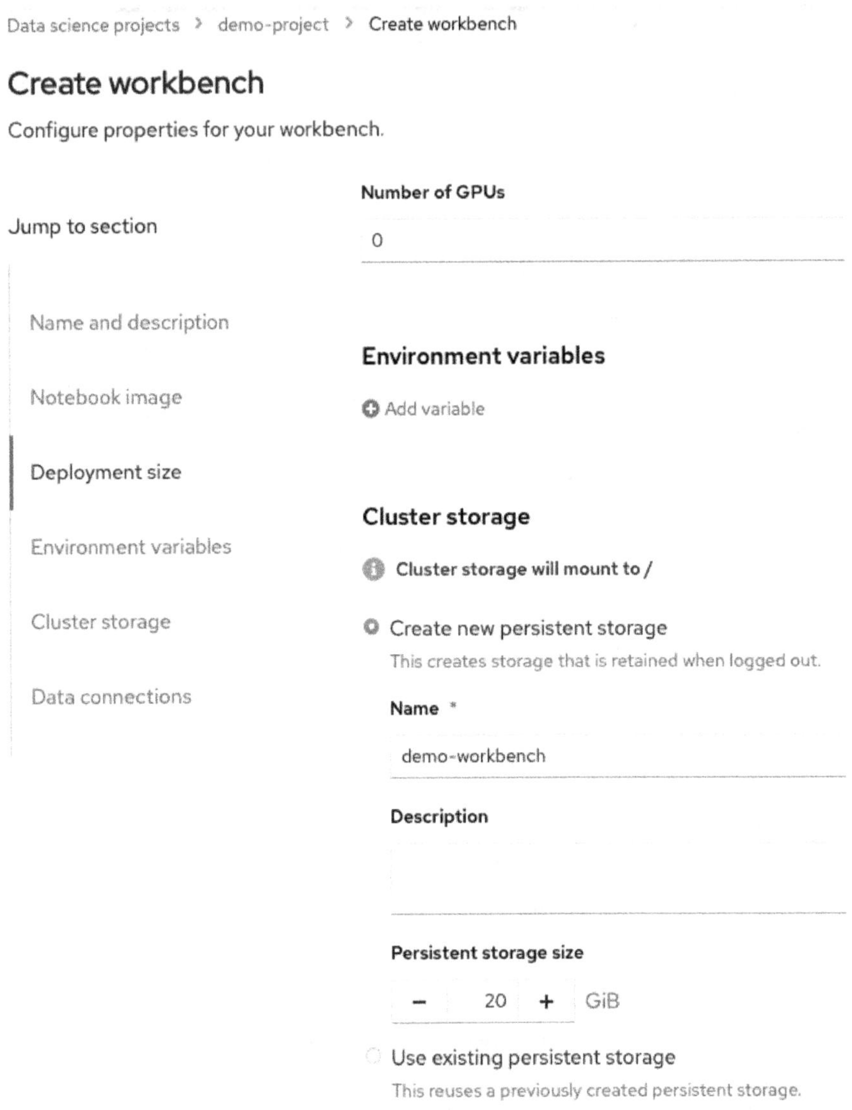

Data science projects > demo-project > Create workbench

Create workbench

Configure properties for your workbench.

Jump to section

Name and description

Notebook image

Deployment size

Environment variables

Cluster storage

Data connections

Number of GPUs

0

Environment variables

⊕ Add variable

Cluster storage

ℹ **Cluster storage will mount to /**

◉ **Create new persistent storage**
This creates storage that is retained when logged out.

Name *

demo-workbench

Description

Persistent storage size

−   20   +   GiB

◯ **Use existing persistent storage**
This reuses a previously created persistent storage.

Figure 3.11 – RHODS – Create workbench

6. Next, you must add a data connection for your development environment to pull/push data from. Go to the **Data Connections** section and add a new one. You will be presented with the following screen, where you can add the connection details to the MinIO bucket that you created earlier in this chapter. Note that AWS_ACCESS_KEY_ID and AWS_SECRET_ACCESS_KEY do not have to be AWS S3 resources. Any S3-compatible component – MinIO, in our case – will do. AWS_S3_ENDPOINT refers to the location of S3, which is the MinIO service you provisioned in the OpenShift ml-workshop project. Add the bucket you created earlier to the

AWS_S3_BUCKET field and select the workbench name **demo-workbench** in the **Connected workbench** dropdown:

```
Name: minio-bucket
AWS_ACCESS_KEY_ID: minio
AWS_SECRET_ACCESS_KEY: minio123
AWS_S3_ENDPOINT: http://minio-ml-workshop.ml-workshop.svc.
cluster.local
AWS_S3_BUCKET: demo-files
Connected workbench: demo-workbench
```

The RHODS platform will inject this information into your workbench environment, as you will see later in this chapter. The screen that contains all this information will look as follows. Click on the **Add data connection** button to save this configuration:

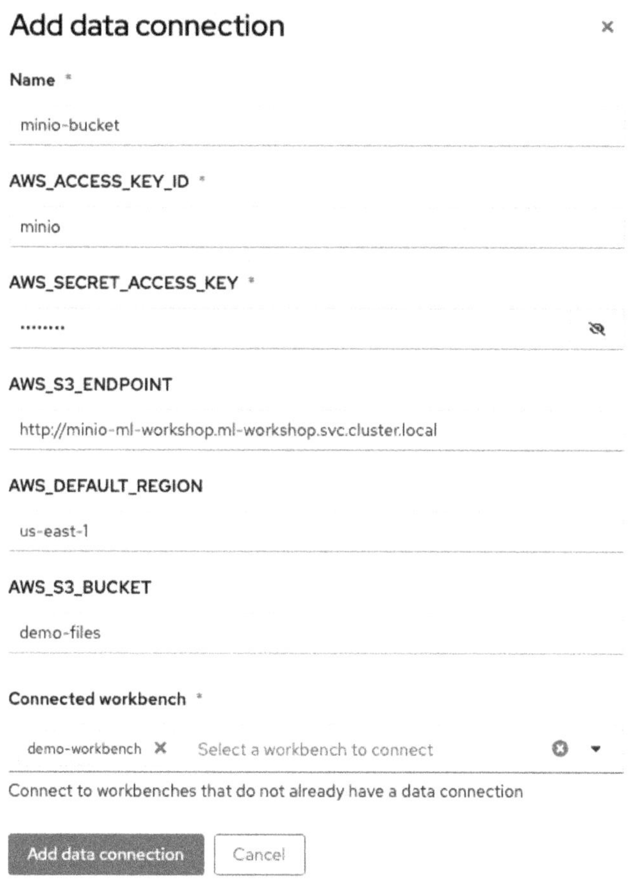

Figure 3.12 – RHODS – Add data connection

7. After you create the project, go to the RHODS landing page, where all the projects are listed, along with the access URL. Click on the workbench link for the project you created earlier:

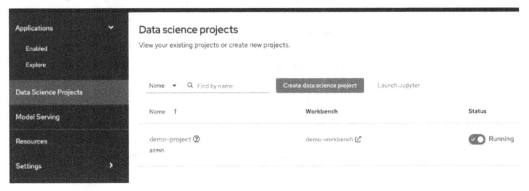

Figure 3.13 – RHODS – List of projects

8. You will be presented with the landing page of your Jupyter Notebook. This environment is created as per the information you provided in *Step 4*. Click on the Python notebook icon to start building:

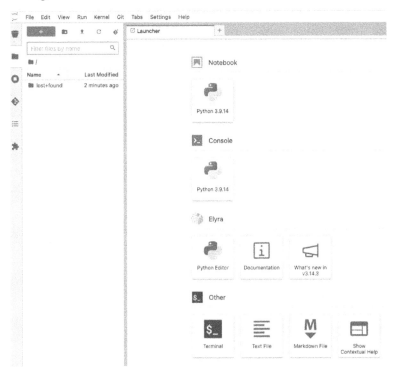

Figure 3.14 – RHODS – Jupyter landing page

9. Validate the environment through a simple print statement, as shown here. Click on the Git icon on the left-hand menu, from where you can clone this book's GitHub repository into your environment:

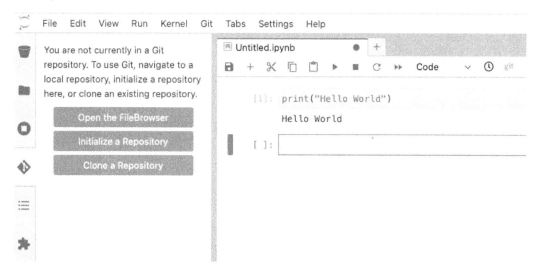

Figure 3.15 – RHODS – Jupyter Notebook

10. Open the `test-s3.py` file from the repository you have just cloned. You will see how the data connection configuration is injected into your environment. Note that variables such as the bucket name are being read from the environment variable, along with other information. The code uses the boto3 library to upload a file onto the S3 bucket that you provisioned earlier. The code creates an empty file named `file.txt` and uploads it to the `demo-files` bucket. Run the notebook:

```
[1]: import boto3, os

     # env variables injected
     # AWS_S3_ENDPOINT=http://minio-ml-workshop.ml-workshop.svc.cluster.local
     # AWS_DEFAULT_REGION=us-east-1
     # AWS_SECRET_ACCESS_KEY=minio123
     # AWS_S3_BUCKET=demo-files
     # AWS_ACCESS_KEY_ID=minio

     BUCKET = os.getenv("AWS_S3_BUCKET")
     HTTP = 'http://'
     AWS_ACCESS_KEY_ID = os.getenv("AWS_ACCESS_KEY_ID")
     AWS_SECRET_ACCESS_KEY = os.getenv("AWS_SECRET_ACCESS_KEY")
     REGIONNAME = os.getenv("AWS_DEFAULT_REGION")
     AWS_S3_ENDPOINT = os.getenv("AWS_S3_ENDPOINT")


     FILENAME_ON_S3 = 'file.txt'
     FILE_ON_DISK = 'file.txt'

     file = open(f"{FILE_ON_DISK}", "w")
     file.write("Hello There \n")
     file.close()

     s3 = boto3.resource('s3',
                 endpoint_url=AWS_S3_ENDPOINT + ":9000",
                 aws_access_key_id=AWS_ACCESS_KEY_ID,
                 aws_secret_access_key=AWS_SECRET_ACCESS_KEY)

     s3.Bucket(BUCKET).upload_file(FILE_ON_DISK, FILENAME_ON_S3)


     print('uploading complete')
     uploading complete
```

Figure 3.16 – RHODS – Python code to upload a file to S3 (MinIO)

11. Once you have executed the notebook, verify that the file has been uploaded onto your bucket by going to the MinIO console. You will see how the file appears in the MinIO console in your **demo-files** bucket:

demo-files
Created on: Tue, May 30 2023 13:38:28 (GMT+10)   Access: PRIVATE

‹   demo-files

▲ Name	Last Modified
📄 file.txt	Today, 13:58

Figure 3.17 – MinIO bucket with files

That is a lot. You have just spawned a development environment on RHODS and started using it for your daily work. The ease of just pointing your browser to the URL and starting to build will enable your team to be agile. The hosted environment brings the benefits of consistency, no more software dependency mismatches between multiple team members, and better security with standard environments.

The RHODS platform also provides an Anaconda server as a commercial offering to run and manage your ML development components. You can provision Anaconda by going to the operators and selecting the Anaconda server. However, we will not cover Anaconda in this book.

Next, we'll learn how to use some of the most popular ML frameworks.

Using ML frameworks in OpenShift

So far, you have seen how easy it is to spin up environments based on your chosen configuration. Red Hat provides a list of pre-built images with popular frameworks to speed up your development workflow. We all know how troublesome it is to maintain multiple runtimes and frameworks with multiple library dependencies. Say you want to start a new environment with TensorFlow. You just select the right container image, as shown in the following screenshot. The **View package information** option provides you with details on what version and library set is available in the container image. The list of available container images is always growing; later, you will learn how to provide custom container images if required:

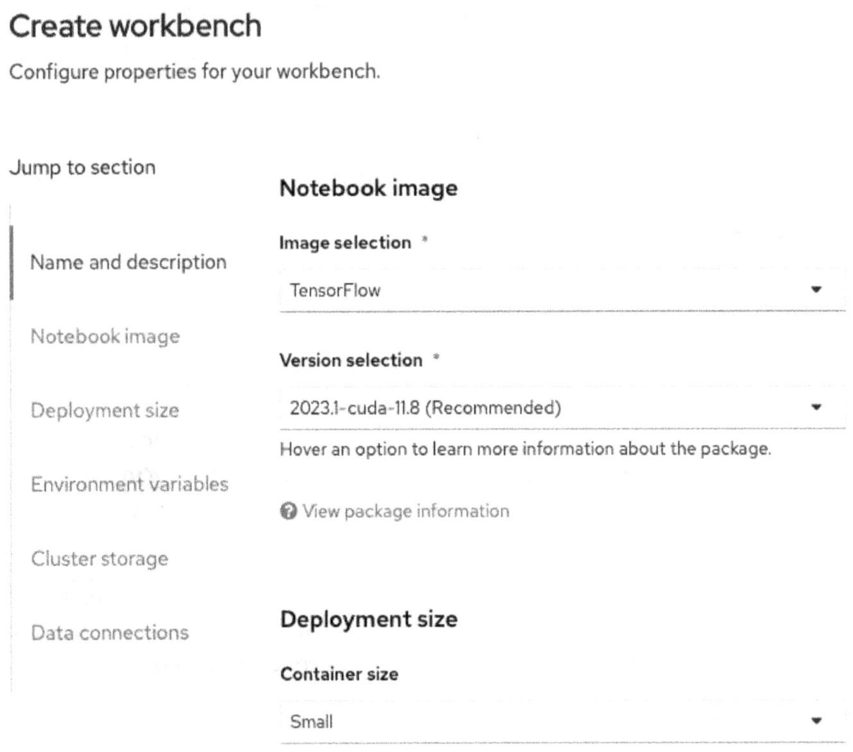

Create workbench

Configure properties for your workbench.

Jump to section

Name and description
Notebook image
Deployment size
Environment variables
Cluster storage
Data connections

Notebook image

Image selection *

| TensorFlow ▼ |

Version selection *

| 2023.1-cuda-11.8 (Recommended) ▼ |

Hover an option to learn more information about the package.

❓ View package information

Deployment size

Container size

| Small ▼ |

Figure 3.18 – RHODS – workbench with TensorFlow image

You may have multiple workbenches with different hardware and software. All these environments are listed under your data science project. You can start and stop environments, where stopping will release the CPU, memory, and any GPU associated, but the disk (cluster storage) will be retained. You can just start the environment again and Red Hat will associate the right disk. However, it is recommended to always push your code to the Git servers. The following screenshot shows how this all information is presented. This one is for a data scientist; everyone will have their own workbenches to train models with ease:

Figure 3.19 – RHODS – project components

With that, you've learned how data scientists can have multiple different environments with hardware and software components without having to build or manage any dependencies for them. It is very easy for your team members to experiment and build models faster. Some ML training may require specialized hardware, such as GPUs. We'll cover this next.

Using GPU acceleration for model training

In the previous section, you customized software components that your team needs to build models. In this section, you will see how RHODS makes it easy for you to use specific hardware for your workbench.

Imagine that you are working on a simple supervised learning model, and you do not need any specific hardware, such as a GPU, to complete your work. If you work on laptops, then the hardware is fixed and shipped with your laptop. You cannot change it dynamically and it would be expensive for organizations to give every data scientist specialized GPU hardware. It's worse if there is a new model of the GPU and you already bought an older version for your team. RHODS enables you to provision hardware on-demand for your team, so if one member needs a GPU, they can just select it from the UI and start using it. Then, when their work is done, the GPU is released back to the hardware pool. This dynamic nature not only reduces costs but also improves the usage of expensive hardware such as GPUs. Let's see how OpenShift allows you to do that.

Enabling GPU support

First, you need to start provisioning nodes with a GPU. Like MinIO, this is a one-time activity that will be executed by the platform engineering team. The entire process of enabling the GPU can be automated for your OpenShift clusters. Let's learn how to provision the machines with a GPU in our cluster.

OpenShift enables you to use **machine sets** to provision nodes – nodes where your container images would run. To enable GPU support for the Jupyter environment that you created earlier, you need to provision nodes with a GPU. Once the nodes with the GPU have been provisioned, RHODS will automatically detect them and allow you to use the Jupyter environment with GPU support.

For the ROSA cluster, you can use the Red Hat cloud console to provision new machines. OpenShift can scale out machines so that it provisions the hardware as needed. You can also choose to use the machine on spot instances to further reduce your bill. Let's see how to add a new machine pool via the Red Hat cloud console:

1. Log in to the Red Hat cloud console and click on **Machine pools**; you will see the following screen. Notice that the name of the cluster will be different for you. Click on the **Add machine pool** button:

Figure 3.20 – The Red Hat cloud console – Machine pools

2. You will see the following screen, where you can select the machine type. Give the machine pool a name such as `gpu-machines` and type in the **Accelerated computing** group in the dropdown. For testing purposes, select the machine with one GPU, as shown here, so that you have minimal costs:

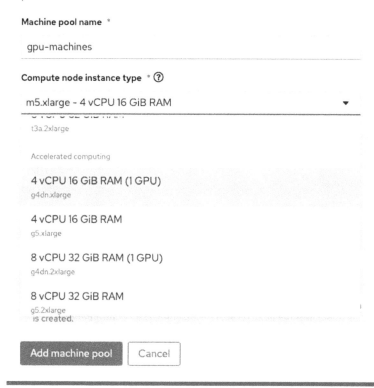

Figure 3.21 – The Red Hat cloud console – machine pool configuration

3.   Once you have selected the right node, add how many nodes you will need. OpenShift allows you to add auto-scaling features, which would be a good fit for any environment. For simplicity, you will not check this box and set **Compute noded count** to **1**. You can also check the spot instance for your workloads, at which point OpenShift will provision the right machine for you. Click the **Add machine pool** button:

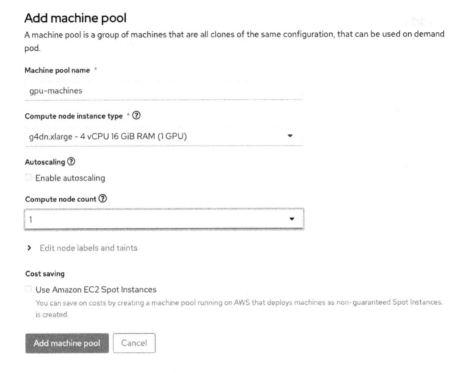

Figure 3.22 – The Red Hat cloud console – machine pool configuration

4. You will see that the newly created machine pool is available in the list below your Red Hat cloud console:

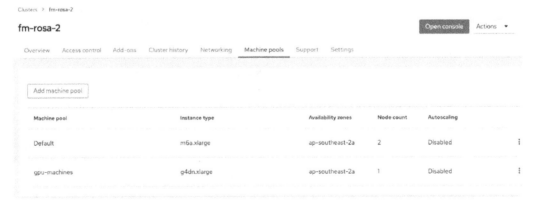

Figure 3.23 – The Red Hat cloud console – machine pools list

At this stage, OpenShift will start provisioning your machine; it will be available in the cluster soon. The next step is to install two bits of software, both of which are delivered using the OpenShift operator framework.

One is **Node Feature Discovery** or simply **NFD**. NFD Operator detects hardware features and configuration in your cluster by labeling the nodes with hardware-specific information such as PCI cards, GPUs, and more.

Second is the NVIDIA GPU operator. The NVIDIA GPU operator automates the management of all NVIDIA software components needed to provision GPU. These components include the NVIDIA drivers, the device plugin for GPUs, NVIDIA Container Runtime, and more.

NFD labels the nodes with hardware and system properties such as PCI cards, and the NVIDIA GPU operator relies on NFD to discover nodes with NVIDIA PCI cards and add more labels to them.

Follow these steps to enable the NFD Operator in your cluster:

1. Log in to the OpenShift console and go to **OperatorHub**. In the search bar on the right-hand side, type NFD:

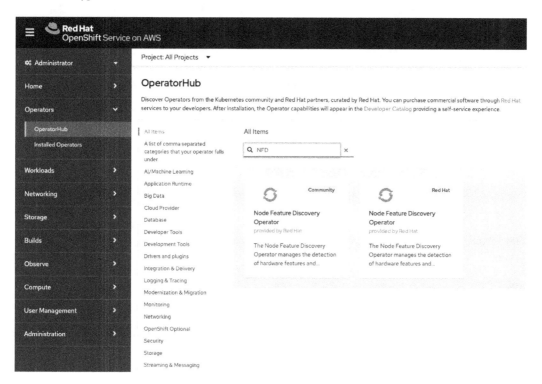

Figure 3.24 – Red Hat OperatorHub – NFD

2. Select the NFD Operator that is provided by Red Hat; you will see the following screen. Click on the **Install** button to start the installation process:

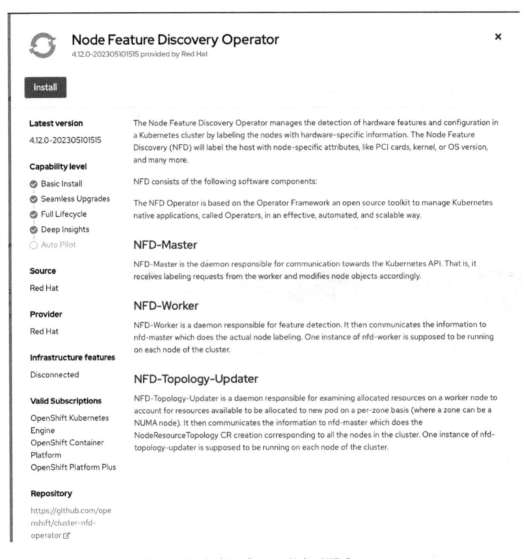

Figure 3.25 – Red Hat OperatorHub – NFD Operator

3. You will get the following screen, where you can configure the operator. Use the default options and click **Install**:

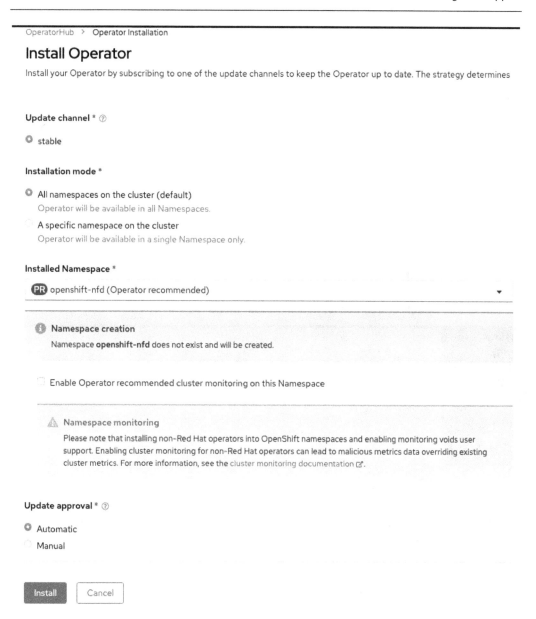

Figure 3.26 – Red Hat OperatorHub – Install Operator

4. You will see the installation's progress. Once the operator has been installed, you will receive confirmation, as shown here:

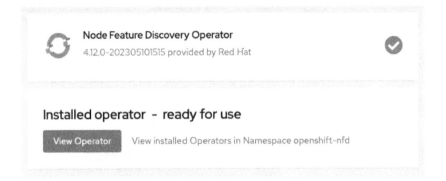

Figure 3.27 – Red Hat OperatorHub – NFD Operator – installation complete

5. NFD Operator has been installed in the opeshift-nfd project. Go to the **Installed Operators** menu and select the **openshift-nfd** project from the dropdown in the right panel. This is where you will create an instance of the operator. Select the **NodeFeatureDiscovery** tab and click on the **Create NodeFeatureDiscovery** button, as shown here:

Figure 3.28 – Red Hat OperatorHub – configuration

6. You will see the following screen. Note that we have trimmed the screen to save space on this page. Use all the default options and click **Create**:

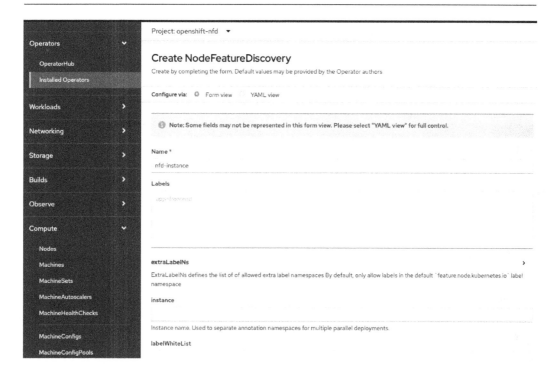

Figure 3.29 - Red Hat OperatorHub – configuration

7.   You will see that the configuration appears in the **NodefeatureDiscovery** tab, as shown here:

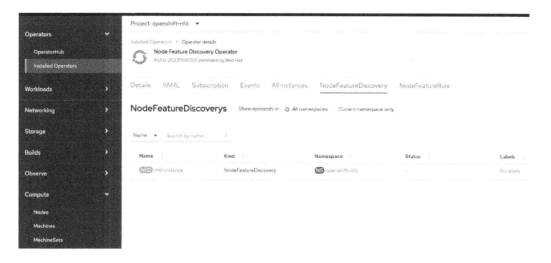

Figure 3.30 – Red Hat OperatorHub – configuration complete

Once you have added the machine pool and installed NFD Operator, the next step is to enable NVIDIA GPU Operator. Follow these steps to install NVIDIA GPU Operator:

1. Log in to the OpenShift console and go to **OperatorHub**. In the search bar on the right-hand side, type `Nvidia`, as shown here. Click on **NVIDIA GPU Operator**:

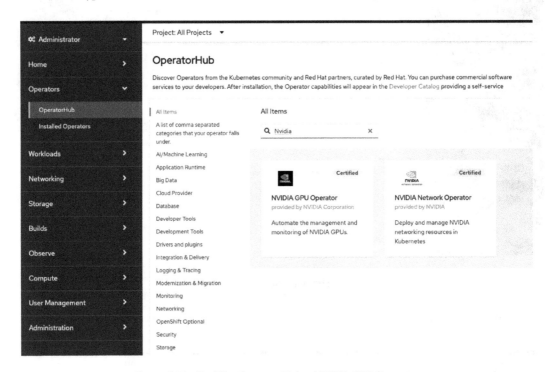

Figure 3.31 – Red Hat OperatorHub – NVIDIA GPU Operator

2. You will get the following screen. Click the **Install** button:

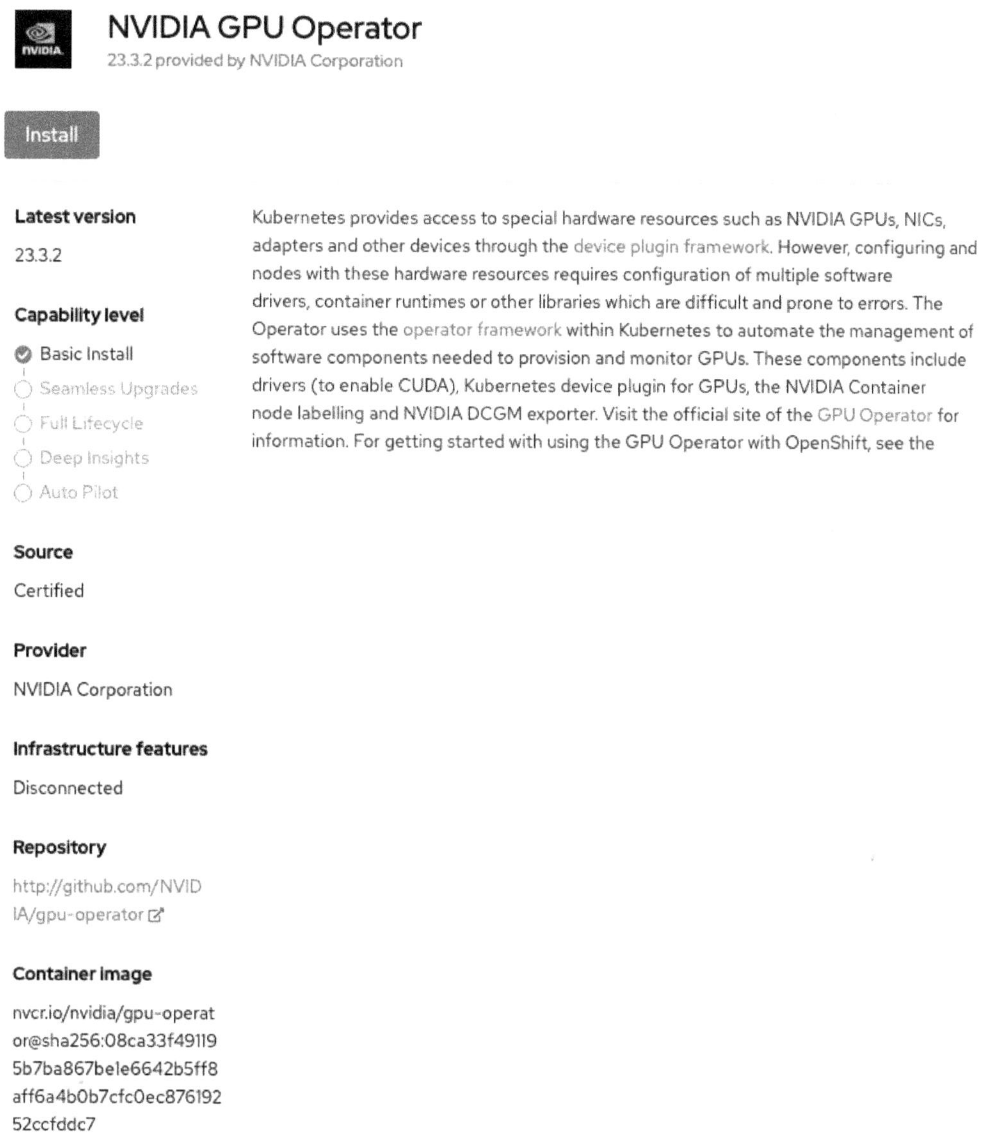

NVIDIA GPU Operator

23.3.2 provided by NVIDIA Corporation

Latest version

23.3.2

Capability level

✅ Basic Install

◯ Seamless Upgrades

◯ Full Lifecycle

◯ Deep Insights

◯ Auto Pilot

Source

Certified

Provider

NVIDIA Corporation

Infrastructure features

Disconnected

Repository

http://github.com/NVID
IA/gpu-operator ☑

Container image

nvcr.io/nvidia/gpu-operat
or@sha256:08ca33f49119
5b7ba867be1e6642b5ff8
aff6a4b0b7cfc0ec876192
52ccfddc7

Kubernetes provides access to special hardware resources such as NVIDIA GPUs, NICs, adapters and other devices through the device plugin framework. However, configuring and nodes with these hardware resources requires configuration of multiple software drivers, container runtimes or other libraries which are difficult and prone to errors. The Operator uses the operator framework within Kubernetes to automate the management of software components needed to provision and monitor GPUs. These components include drivers (to enable CUDA), Kubernetes device plugin for GPUs, the NVIDIA Container node labelling and NVIDIA DCGM exporter. Visit the official site of the GPU Operator for information. For getting started with using the GPU Operator with OpenShift, see the

Figure 3.32 – Red Hat OperatorHub – NVIDIA GPU Operator

3. You will get the following screen. Use the default options and click on the **Install** button. Note that the operator will be installed into the nvidia-gpu-operator project:

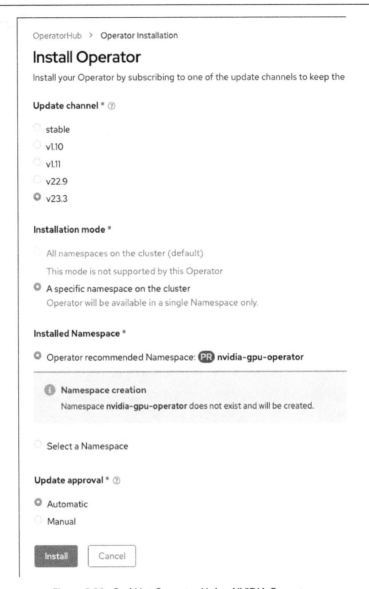

Figure 3.33 - Red Hat Operator Hub – NVIDIA Operator

4. You will see the installation's progress. Once the operator has been installed, you will get confirmation of this, as shown here:

Figure 3.34 – Red Hat OperatorHub – NVIDIA GPU Operator – installation complete

5. NVIDIA GPU Operator will be installed in the `nvidia-gpu-operator` project. Go to the **Installed Operators** menu and select the **nvidia-gpu-operator** project from the dropdown in the right panel. This is where you will be creating an instance of the operator. Select the **ClusterPolicy** tab and click on the **Create ClusterPolicy** button, as shown here:

Figure 3.35 – Red Hat OperatorHub – NVIDIA GPU Operator – configuration

6. Create the configuration with all the default options:

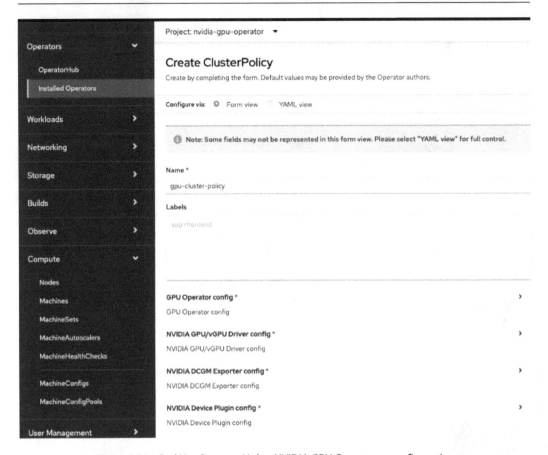

Figure 3.36 – Red Hat OperatorHub – NVIDIA GPU Operator – configuration

7. Go to the same **ClusterPolicy** tab and verify that the instance you have created is available here:

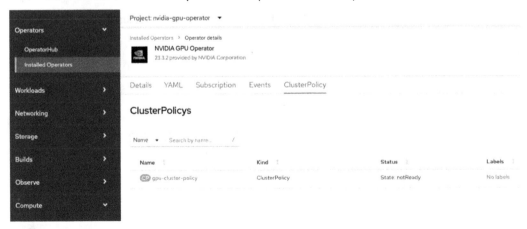

Figure 3.37 – Red Hat OperatorHub – NVIDIA GPU Operator – configuration complete

This finishes the configuration part for the GPU hardware. Notice that all these steps for installing and configuring machine sets for NFD Operator and NVIDIA GPU Operator can be fully automated. We have chosen to use the UI-based approach so that you understand the process better.

Finally, verify that your machines have been added and labeled correctly by the operators. Go to the OpenShift console and under the **Compute** left-hand menu, select **Machines**. Then, in the right-hand panel, search for gpu in the search box, as shown in the following screenshot. Remember that when you created the machine set in the Red Hat console, you called it gpu-machines; that is the first few characters of what we are searching for. As you can see, one machine has been found (because we kept the node count to 1 in the machine set configuration in the Red Hat cloud console).

OpenShift can automatically add more machines and retire them as the load varies. The operators install the required software on the new machines provisioned by the OpenShift platform:

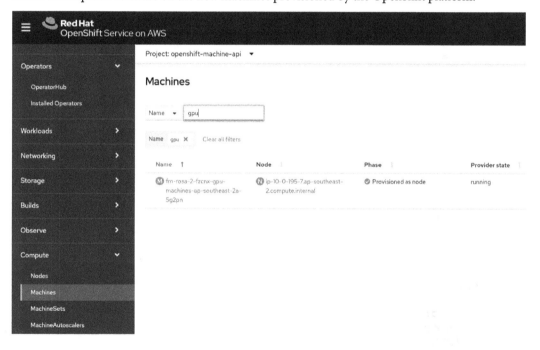

Figure 3.38 – Red Hat OpenShift – GPU machines

After setting up these components, which can be fully automated, the data science team will use the resources as required. All the data scientists have to do is go to the **Create workbench** screen of RHODS and create a new workbench; the **GPU** dropdown will appear with the maximum number of GPUs available to use. Select the **TensorFlow** notebook image with CUDA for **Deployment size** and set **Number of GPUs** to **1**, as shown here. Then, start this workbench:

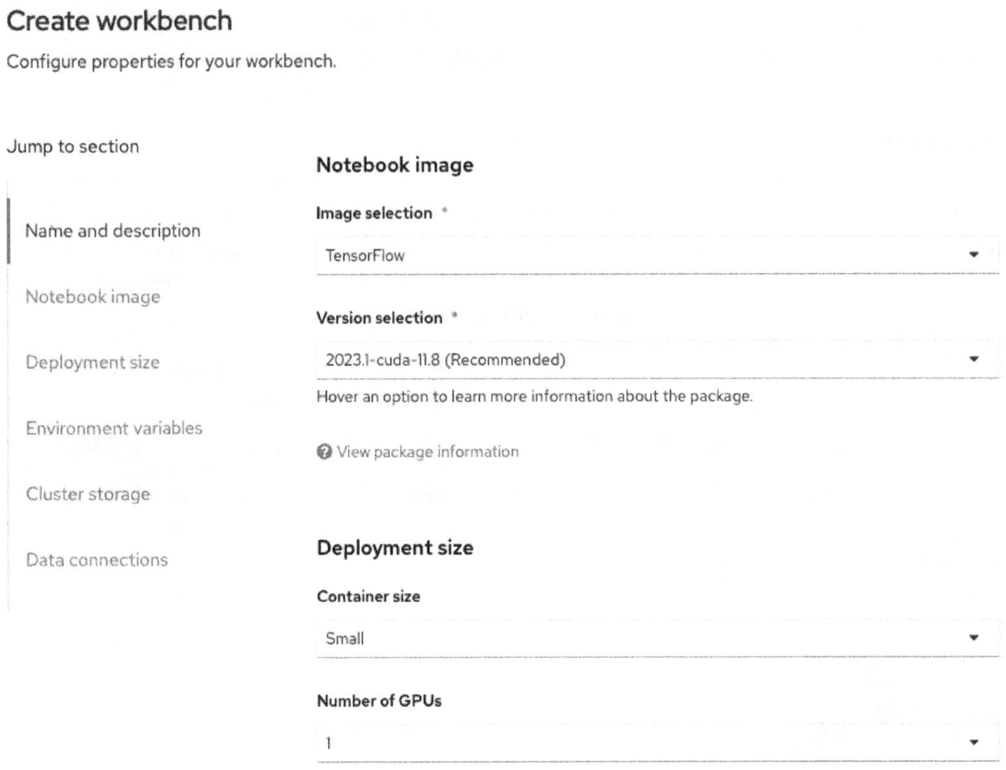

Create workbench

Configure properties for your workbench.

Jump to section

Name and description

Notebook image

Deployment size

Environment variables

Cluster storage

Data connections

Notebook image

Image selection *

TensorFlow

Version selection *

2023.1-cuda-11.8 (Recommended)

Hover an option to learn more information about the package.

❔ View package information

Deployment size

Container size

Small

Number of GPUs

1

Figure 3.39 – Red Hat OpenShift – creating a notebook with a GPU

Once you have started the workbench, you can run the following code to validate that the GPU is accessible for you to use. If someone else in your team tries to start another workbench with GPU support, they will not be able to do it because OpenShift knows that the GPU is in use:

```
import tensorflow as tf
print("Num GPUs Available: ", len(tf.config.list_physical_
devices('GPU')))
```

The output of this code will show the number of GPUs that you can use:

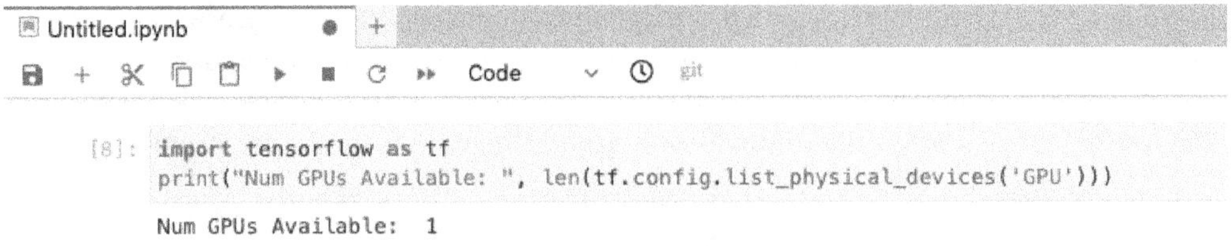

```
[8]: import tensorflow as tf
     print("Num GPUs Available: ", len(tf.config.list_physical_devices('GPU')))

     Num GPUs Available:  1
```

Figure 3.40 – Notebook with GPU

With that, you've seen how easy it is to use different hardware and software using the capabilities of OpenShift. The team has a consistent environment with the right set of hardware available for the whole team. RHODS simplifies your model development flow by providing the necessary management for the hardware and software your organization needs during model development.

In the next section, you will learn how to extend the OpenShift-provided container images with your custom ones. You may have specific additional libraries, or you may want to add public certificates for your environment so that the notebooks can make SSL calls.

Building custom notebooks

Though RHODS comes with a few in-built notebooks that you can use, you may require a different library version and/or dependency, or you may want to add your organization certificates to the notebook. The point is there can be many reasons why the provided notebooks may require some tuning.

In this section, you will learn how to tune the existing notebook images, import third-party notebook images, and create your custom notebook images.

RHODS allows you to bring notebook images into the platform, either by importing an existing container image from a registry such as DockerHub, Quay, or any other container registry, or by customizing an existing notebook image. Let's look at how to create custom notebook images and import them into RHODS.

Creating a custom notebook image

Creating custom notebook images follows a standard container image build process. This involves creating a *Dockerfile* that describes how the container image is to be built.

Follow these steps to build your custom notebook image. You will need *Docker* or *Podman* installed on your machine. We will use Docker for this example:

1. In this book's GitHub repository, we have prepared an example *Dockerfile* that will build a custom notebook image. Navigate to the `chapter3/custom-notebook-image` directory.

2. Run the following command:

    ```
    docker build --platform linux/amd64 -t custom-notebook-python3.9
    .
    ```

    This will start the Docker image build.

3. Once the build is successful, you should be able to create a container from this image that will run a JupyterLab notebook in your local environment, as shown in *Figure 3.41*. Run the following command to run the container:

    ```
    docker run -p 8888:8888 custom-notebook-python3.9
    ```

The screenshot below captures the output of the command above.

```
ross@Rosss-Mac-Studio custom-notebook-image % docker run -p 8888:8888 custom-notebook-python3.9
WARNING: The requested image's platform (linux/amd64) does not match the detected host platform (linux/arm64/v8) and no spe
cific platform was requested
Running command: jupyter lab --ServerApp.root_dir=/opt/app-root/src --ServerApp.ip=0.0.0.0 --ServerApp.allow_origin=* --Ser
verApp.open_browser=False
[I 2023-06-19 17:37:28.339 ServerApp] jupyter_server_mathjax | extension was successfully linked.
[I 2023-06-19 17:37:28.340 ServerApp] jupyter_server_proxy | extension was successfully linked.
[I 2023-06-19 17:37:28.361 ServerApp] jupyter_server_terminals | extension was successfully linked.
[I 2023-06-19 17:37:28.386 ServerApp] jupyterlab | extension was successfully linked.
[I 2023-06-19 17:37:28.387 ServerApp] jupyterlab_git | extension was successfully linked.
[I 2023-06-19 17:37:28.410 ServerApp] nbclassic | extension was successfully linked.
[I 2023-06-19 17:37:28.411 ServerApp] nbdime | extension was successfully linked.
[I 2023-06-19 17:37:28.411 ServerApp] nbgitpuller | extension was successfully linked.
[I 2023-06-19 17:37:28.416 ServerApp] Writing Jupyter server cookie secret to /opt/app-root/src/.local/share/jupyter/runtim
e/jupyter_cookie_secret
[I 2023-06-19 17:37:29.214 ServerApp] notebook_shim | extension was successfully linked.
[I 2023-06-19 17:37:29.317 ServerApp] notebook_shim | extension was successfully loaded.
[I 2023-06-19 17:37:29.320 ServerApp] jupyter_server_mathjax | extension was successfully loaded.
[I 2023-06-19 17:37:29.364 ServerApp] jupyter_server_proxy | extension was successfully loaded.
[I 2023-06-19 17:37:29.368 ServerApp] jupyter_server_terminals | extension was successfully loaded.
[I 2023-06-19 17:37:29.370 LabApp] JupyterLab extension loaded from /opt/app-root/lib64/python3.9/site-packages/jupyterlab
[I 2023-06-19 17:37:29.371 LabApp] JupyterLab application directory is /opt/app-root/share/jupyter/lab
[I 2023-06-19 17:37:29.385 ServerApp] jupyterlab | extension was successfully loaded.
[I 2023-06-19 17:37:29.412 ServerApp] jupyterlab_git | extension was successfully loaded.
[I 2023-06-19 17:37:29.428 ServerApp] nbclassic | extension was successfully loaded.
[I 2023-06-19 17:37:29.658 ServerApp] nbdime | extension was successfully loaded.
[I 2023-06-19 17:37:29.660 ServerApp] nbgitpuller | extension was successfully loaded.
[I 2023-06-19 17:37:29.663 ServerApp] Serving notebooks from local directory: /opt/app-root/src
[I 2023-06-19 17:37:29.663 ServerApp] Jupyter Server 2.1.0 is running at:
[I 2023-06-19 17:37:29.663 ServerApp] http://07c74a4a6f84:8888/lab?token=d3d80cd68fedb641b00107b577e4f0fc10addbddc1f05f3b
[I 2023-06-19 17:37:29.663 ServerApp]  or http://127.0.0.1:8888/lab?token=d3d80cd68fedb641b00107b577e4f0fc10addbddc1f05f3b
[I 2023-06-19 17:37:29.663 ServerApp] Use Control-C to stop this server and shut down all kernels (twice to skip confirmati
on).
[C 2023-06-19 17:37:29.679 ServerApp]

    To access the server, open this file in a browser:
        file:///opt/app-root/src/.local/share/jupyter/runtime/jpserver-9-open.html
    Or copy and paste one of these URLs:
        http://07c74a4a6f84:8888/lab?token=d3d80cd68fedb641b00107b577e4f0fc10addbddc1f05f3b
     or http://127.0.0.1:8888/lab?token=d3d80cd68fedb641b00107b577e4f0fc10addbddc1f05f3b
```

Figure 3.41 – Output of the docker run command

4.   To validate whether the container is working, open `http://localhost:8888` in your browser. You should see the JupyterLab setup page, as shown in *Figure 3.42*:

Figure 3.42 – The JupyterLab landing page

5. Now that you've verified that the container image is working, you can push this image to an image registry. For this example, we will push this to Docker Hub. Run the following commands to push this to your Docker Hub repository:

```
docker tag custom-notebook-python3.9 <DOCKER_HUB_
USERNAME>/custom-notebook-python3.9:latest
docker push <DOCKER_HUB_USERNAME>/custom-notebook-
python3.9:latest
```

Replace <DOCKER_HUB_USERNAME> with your Docker Hub username or repository name.

With that, you have successfully published a customer *JupyterLab* notebook container image to an image registry. The version of this *Dockerfile* must be managed through standard DevOps practices, which includes a configuration management system such as Git, a CI/CD pipeline, and proper release management.

Now, let's learn how to use the published custom notebook container image.

Importing notebook images

Now that you have a custom notebook container image published in DockerHub, you can import this image into RHODS by following these steps:

1. In the **OpenShift Data Science** console, navigate to **Settings | Notebook Images** and click the **Import image** button, as shown in *Figure 3.43*:

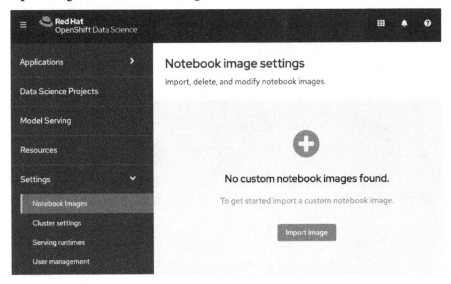

Figure 3.43 – Notebook image settings

2. Let's import the custom notebook image that we published to *Docker Hub* in the previous section. Set the repository to the image repository URL of your customer notebook image, as shown in *Figure 3.44*. Then, click the **Import** button:

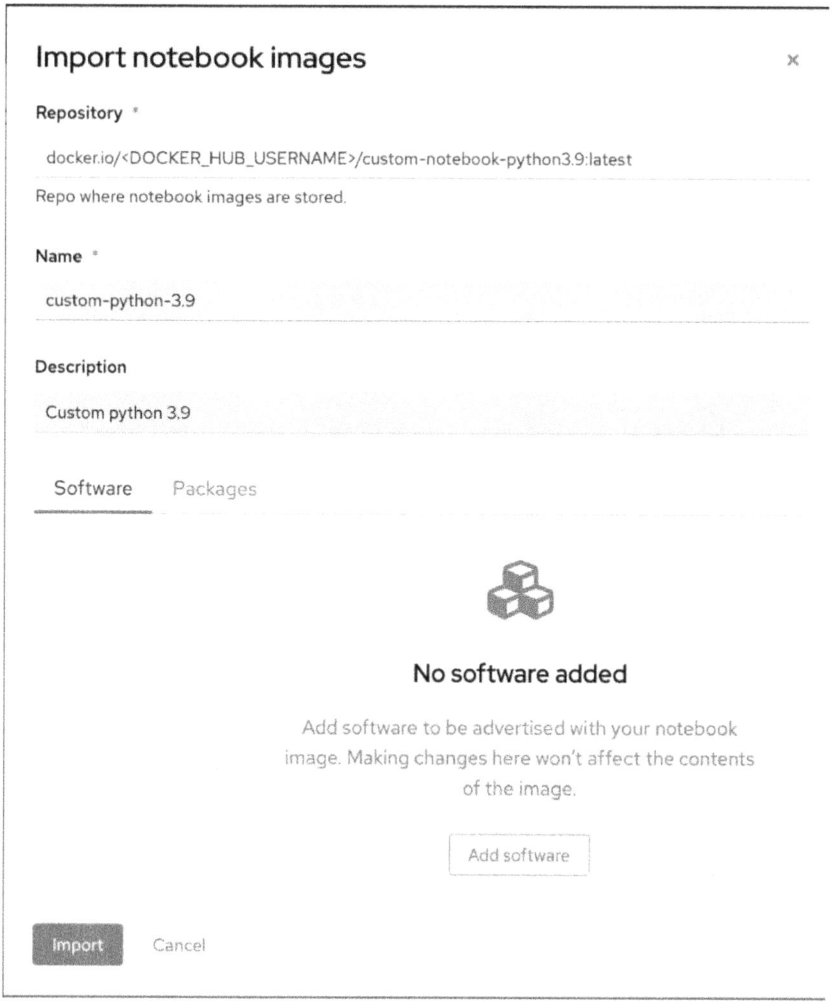

Figure 3.44 – Import notebook images

3. You have just imported your custom notebook container image into RHODS. You can use this to create new workbenches. The new notebook image will appear in the image selection list when you're creating a workbench, as shown in *Figure 3.45*:

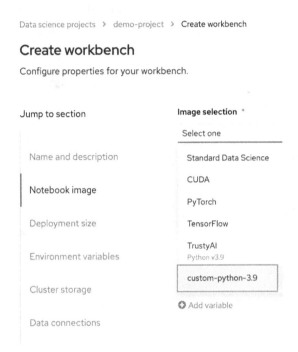

Figure 3.45 – The image selection list showing the new notebook image

Congratulations! You have successfully created a custom notebook image, published the image to Docker Hub, and imported the published image into RHODS. The same steps apply to image registries other than **Docker Hub**.

You can now create new workbenches using your custom notebook image.

Summary

In this chapter, you learned how to use the core features of RHODS. You learned how to create and manage data science projects, workbenches, storage, and data connections.

You also saw how RHODS does the heavy lifting for hardware and software provisioning for your model development workflow. This includes learning how to take advantage of GPUs through machine pools. This dynamic model development environment enables your team to be more agile and focus on model building instead of managing the libraries.

Finally, you learned how to extend the base images to create a set of environments that is more suited to your needs. There, you learned how to create and use custom notebook images in RHODS. This allows you to further customize and tailor the experiences of your data science team.

In the next chapter, you will learn how to build and package ML models for consumption.

Part 3: Operating ML Workloads

This part covers the operational aspects of MLOps, including building pipelines for training and deployment automation and model serving.

This part has the following chapters:

- *Chapter 4, Managing a Model Training Workflow*
- *Chapter 5, Deploying ML Models as a Service*
- *Chapter 6, Operating ML Workloads*
- *Chapter 7, Building a Face Detector Using the Red Hat ML Platform*

4

Managing a Model Training Workflow

You created a data science project and a workbench created in **OpenShift Data Science** (**ODS**) in the previous chapter. In this chapter, you will learn how to build a model training pipeline. You will see how you can version your data using the partner software available in Red Hat OpenShift and build automated pipelines to retrain your model as new data becomes available. You will use the Jupyter notebook that you have configured in your workbench and write Python code to build a simple **machine learning** (**ML**) model.

It is important to understand how to manually embed a model into an application before we introduce you to the concept of model serving. We will take you through the following sections in this chapter:

- Configuring Pachyderm
- Versioning your data with Pachyderm
- Training a model using Red Hat ODS
- Building a model training pipeline

Technical requirements

In this chapter, you need to use the accompanying GitHub repository of this book. This can be found at `https://github.com/PacktPublishing/MLOps-with-Red-Hat-OpenShift`. The files you will need are in the directory named `chapter4`. You will also write basic Python code to build a basic model and a model training pipeline.

Configuring Pachyderm

Let's start by configuring Pachyderm. Pachyderm is a platform that assists data scientists in creating complete ML workflows covering all the stages from data ingestion and model training up to deploying into production. Think of it as a version control system (VCS) for your model development workflow.

In traditional software engineering, you may use Git to version control your code. In ML projects, you need to version control your data, and you want a reproducible flow for training your model. Pachyderm provides such capabilities for you. You will see how Red Hat OpenShift enables you to use Pachyderm. Refer to *Chapter 3* for instructions on installing the Pachyderm operator.

Follow these steps to configure Pachyderm. Pachyderm needs a **relational database management system** (**RDBMS**) to store metadata, and the operator takes care of the Pachyderm and related database components. Pachyderm requires **Simple Storage Service** (**S3**) storage to store the **Pachyderm File System** (**PFS**) and the pipeline-related files. It supports any S3 object storage, and in this book, you will configure it to use the MinIO server you provisioned in *Chapter 3*:

1. Create a bucket named `pachyderm` in the MinIO server of your OpenShift cluster:

Figure 4.1 – Bucket for Pachyderm

2. Create a new project named `pachyderm` in your OpenShift cluster.
3. From the OpenShift console, select **Installed Operators** and select your newly created project. Then, click on the **Pachyderm** tab in the right panel:

Figure 4.2 – Pachyderm server creation

4. Now, you will create a new Pachyderm instance by clicking on the **Create Pachyderm** button. Select the **YAML view** radio button and paste the configuration available in the Git repo of this book. The filename is `chapter4/pachyderm.yaml`. Hit the **Create** button once you've finished making your changes:

Figure 4.3 – Pachyderm server creation

Notice lines *21* to *30* where the configuration of your MinIO server has been set. Make changes as per your environment. You can see the configuration in the following code snippet, especially the `bucket` and `endpoint` properties:

```
storage:
backend: MINIO
minio:
bucket: pachyderm
endpoint: 'minio-ml-workshop.minio.svc.cluster.local:9000'
id: minio
secret: minio123
secure: 'false'
putFileConcurrencyLimit: 100
uploadFileConcurrencyLimit: 100
```

5. Once the installation is complete, you should see the **Running** status, as shown in *Figure 4.4*:

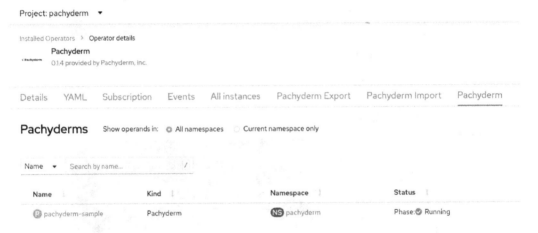

Figure 4.4 – Pachyderm instance showing Running status

6. Navigate to the **Red Hat OpenShift Data Science** page by clicking on the `rhods-dashboard` route in the `redhat-ods-applications` project. You will see that Pachyderm is now displayed as an installed component in the dashboard, as shown next:

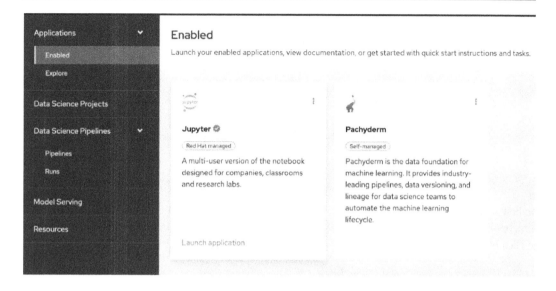

Figure 4.5 – Pachyderm displayed as an enabled component in the dashboard

Congratulations! You have just installed an instance of the Pachyderm server. In the next section, we will show you how to version your datasets using the Pachyderm server.

Versioning your data with Pachyderm

Data is the fundamental component for building your models. Without a retrievable version of the dataset the model was trained on, you cannot replicate the model training activity you did in the past and expect the same results. Data versioning enables dataset comparisons and prevents confusion that may occur due to data changes. This allows us to build a reproducible model training workflow. To learn more about Pachyderm in depth, refer to the Pachyderm documentation at https:// docs.pachyderm.com/.

To work with Pachyderm, you can either use the Pachyderm command-line tool, pachctl, or the Pachyderm Python library, which we will use in this book.

Before we start, let's create a new bucket in your MinIO server. We will use this to store the datasets. Let's call this bucket raw-data. Then, upload the wine.csv file available in the Git repository of this book into this bucket. For the purpose of this exercise, set the raw-data bucket as **Public** in the MinIO server, as shown next:

Figure 4.6 – Setting the raw-data bucket as Public

The first step is to start a new Jupyter notebook using the **Standard Data Science** notebook image. Then, open the notebook provided in `chapter4/multi-version.ipynb`. Let's go through each cell of the notebook to understand how you can version your data with Pachyderm.

The first two cells are where you install the Python libraries for Pachyderm and make the imports:

```
!pip install python-pachyderm
import python_pachyderm as pc
```

The next step is to connect to the Pachyderm server you configured earlier in this chapter. The Pachyderm server instance is internally exposed as a service in OpenShift at `pachd.pachyderm.svc.cluster.local`. It uses the OpenShift service naming, with `pachyderm` as the name of the project where you have installed the Pachyderm service:

```
client = pc.Client(host="pachd.pachyderm.svc.cluster.local")
```

Just as in Git version control, you start by creating a repository for your project. For this example, we create the repository named `multiple_version`. We have included and commented out the code for deleting repositories if you need to delete your Pachyderm repo for any reason:

```
# client.delete_repo("multiple_version")
client.create_repo("multiple_version")
```

The next step is to create a file and store it in the Pachyderm repository. You commit the file in the `multiple_version` repository in the master branch and provide a description of the commit message. The `put_file_bytes()` function takes the file data and location to store the file in PFS.

Take note of the commit ID to refer to it in the later steps. You do not need to save the commit ID, and you can list all the commits available:

```
first_commit_id = ""
with client.commit("multiple_version", "master", \
    description="commit message") as commit:
    client.put_file_bytes(commit, "/dir_a/data.txt", b"DATA")
    print(commit.id)
    first_commit_id = commit.id
```

Now, overwrite the same file with new data. Pachyderm will create a new version of the file with a new commit ID. Notice that the commit ID in this version is different from the previous version:

```
with client.commit("multiple_version", "master") as commit:
    client.put_file_bytes(commit, "/dir_a/data.txt", b"DATAV2")
    print(commit.id)
```

If you now get the file from the Pachyderm repository, you will get the latest version, as you can see next. The output of the following code will be DATAV2, which is the data in the latest version of this file:

```
f = client.get_file(("multiple_version", "master"), "/dir_a/data.txt")
print(f.read())
```

You can, however, get a specific version of the file too by providing the commit ID, as shown next. The first_commit_id variable stores the commit ID of the first version of the data file. The output of the following code would be DATA:

```
f = client.get_file(("multiple_version", "master", \
    first_commit_id), "/dir_a/data.txt")
print(f.read())
```

You do not always need to provide the data as bytes; you can also refer to the original file location as a URL, as shown next. In the following code snippet, the wine.csv file is recorded into the Pachyderm file server:

```
with client.commit("multiple_version", "master") as commit:
    client.put_file_url(commit, 'wine.csv', \
        'http://minio-ml-workshop.minio.svc.cluster.local:9000/raw-
data/wine.csv')
    print(commit.id)
```

The complete notebook is shown in *Figure 4.7*:

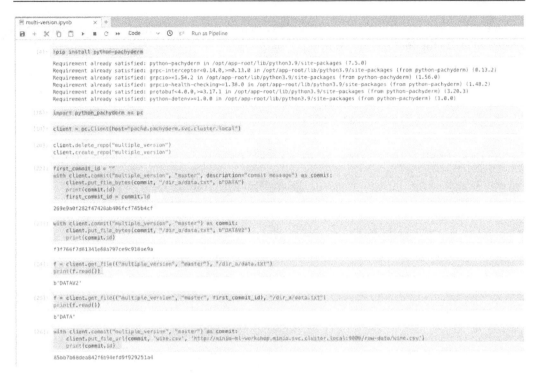

Figure 4.7 – Notebook for experimenting with data versioning

You have seen how Pachyderm enables you to version your data and helps you build reproducible ML workflows. Red Hat OpenShift makes it easy to operate and integrate Pachyderm at scale so that you can focus on building valuable models.

In the next section, we will show you how you can use Red Hat ODS to build a model.

Training a model using Red Hat ODS

Let's build a simple model using Red Hat ODS. Recall *Chapter 3, Building Machine Learning models with OpenShift*, and create a new data science project named `wines`. Create a workbench named `wines` inside the project using the **Standard Data Science** notebook image and a **Small** container size. Create new persistence storage named `wines` with 20 GB of storage. There is no need to create a data connection at this stage. Once you create this project, you will have the following screen for your project:

Figure 4.8 – Red Hat data science project

1. Now, launch the notebook and clone the accompanying Git repository of this book. Use the chapter4/wine-data-version.ipynb file to create a version of the wines.csv file in the Pachyderm repo. Note the commit ID while running this notebook.

2. Once you have executed this notebook, open chapter4/wine-training.ipynb to train a simple linear regression model. Let's go through this notebook step by step.

3. First, you define a commit ID variable to pull the data from the Pachyderm repo. Then, you will connect to the Pachyderm server and load the data into a pandas DataFrame. The following code refers to these steps.

4. Note that the commit ID will be different in your setup, and you need to change it as per your last commit ID:

```
commit_id = "be82b14369c74ff7bbdf9866d6f701ee"
import python_pachyderm as pc
client = pc.Client(host="pachd.pachyderm.svc.cluster.local")
import pandas as pd
wines = client.get_file(("wines", "master", \
    commit_id), "wine.csv")
wines_df = pd.read_csv(wines, delimiter=';')
```

5. Now that the versioned data is loaded, we can split the dataset into training and test datasets:

```
# Split data into training and test
wine_train = wines_df.sample(frac=0.7)
print(wine_train.shape)
wine_test = wines_df.loc[\
    ~wines_df.set_index( \
        list(wines_df.columns) \
    ).index.isin(wine_train.set_index( \
        list(wine_train.columns)).index)]
print(wine_test.shape)
```

6. Next is to train the model using linear regression:

```
from sklearn.linear_model import LinearRegression
features = ['volatile acidity', 'residual sugar', \
    'chlorides', 'total sulfur dioxide', 'sulphates',\
    'alcohol']
wine_ln_reg = LinearRegression()
wine_ln_reg = wine_ln_reg.fit(wine_train[features], \
    wine_train['quality'])
```

The complete notebook has graphs to validate your model; we encourage you to investigate it and enhance the notebook as needed.

Data scientists usually run the notebook's cells many times throughout the experiment while tweaking parameters. Next is to build a pipeline that will automate this process for reproducibility and automation.

Building a model training pipeline

Red Hat OpenShift pipelines automate training and deployment workflows. They are based on the Kubeflow pipeline **domain-specific language** (**DSL**) and backed by the Tekton engine. In this section, you will build a pipeline from the notebook you created earlier. In the next chapters, you will add more stages to this pipeline.

Installing Red Hat OpenShift Pipelines

This is a familiar process where you log in to OpenShift, select the right operator, and perform an install. Follow the next steps to install the pipeline operator:

1. Log in to the OpenShift console and search for **OpenShift Pipelines** from OperatorHub, as shown in *Figure 4.9*. Click on the **Red Hat OpenShift Pipelines** tile:

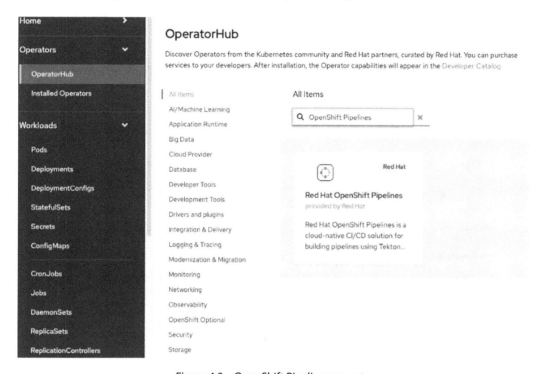

Figure 4.9 – OpenShift Pipelines operator

2. Using all the default options, click on the **Install** button, as shown in *Figure 4.10*:

> **Note**
>
> The version of the operator may have already changed by the time you are reading this. Use the latest version that is available in your OpenShift instance.

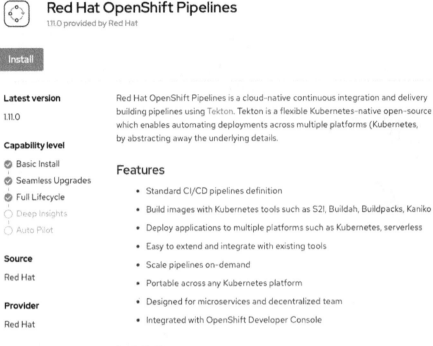

Red Hat OpenShift Pipelines

1.11.0 provided by Red Hat

Install

Latest version

1.11.0

Capability level

✓ Basic Install

✓ Seamless Upgrades

✓ Full Lifecycle

○ Deep Insights

○ Auto Pilot

Source

Red Hat

Provider

Red Hat

Infrastructure features

Disconnected

Proxy-aware

Valid Subscriptions

OpenShift Container Platform

OpenShift Platform Plus

Red Hat OpenShift Pipelines is a cloud-native continuous integration and delivery building pipelines using Tekton. Tekton is a flexible Kubernetes-native open-source which enables automating deployments across multiple platforms (Kubernetes, by abstracting away the underlying details.

Features

- Standard CI/CD pipelines definition
- Build images with Kubernetes tools such as S2I, Buildah, Buildpacks, Kaniko
- Deploy applications to multiple platforms such as Kubernetes, serverless
- Easy to extend and integrate with existing tools
- Scale pipelines on-demand
- Portable across any Kubernetes platform
- Designed for microservices and decentralized team
- Integrated with OpenShift Developer Console

Installation

Red Hat OpenShift Pipelines Operator gets installed into a single namespace which would then install *Red Hat OpenShift Pipelines* into the openshift-pipelines *OpenShift Pipelines* is however cluster-wide and can run pipelines created in any

Components

- Tekton Pipelines: v0.47.2
- Tekton Triggers: v0.24.1

Figure 4.10 – Red Hat OpenShift Pipelines operator install screen

3.   The screen in *Figure 4.11* will present an opportunity to change the namespaces, use the default namespace, and click the **Install** button:

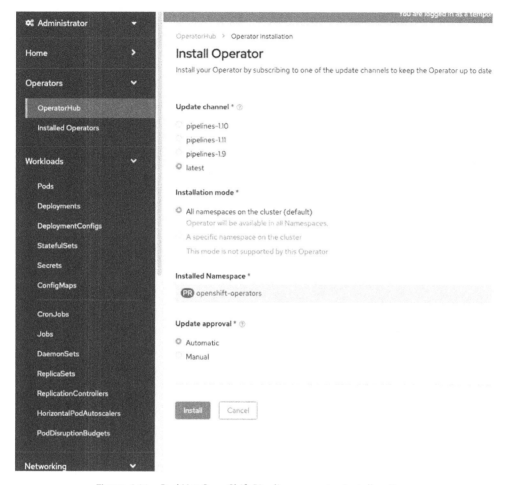

Figure 4.11 – Red Hat OpenShift Pipelines operator install options

4. Wait for the operator to be installed, and you are good to go.

Once the installation is complete, we must attach a pipeline server to your data science project.

Attaching a pipeline server to your project

In order to run data pipelines and training pipelines within your ODS project, you need to create a pipeline server attached to your ODS project.

Now, create and attach the pipeline server to your data science project. A Tekton pipeline server will be created and associated with your data science project. The attached pipeline server will host and execute the pipeline jobs of your data science project.

> **Note**
>
> **Data science project** is an OpenShift namespace, and you can go through the OpenShift console to see different components installed in the namespace to verify the pipeline server installation.

The following steps will attach a pipeline server to your data science project:

1. Create a bucket named `pipelines` in your MinIO server.

2. Open your Red Hat data science project and click on the **Create a pipeline server** button, as shown in *Figure 4.12*:

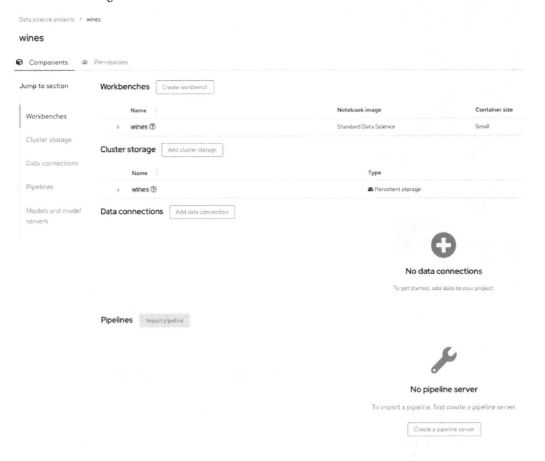

Figure 4.12 – Creating a pipeline server in the data science project

3. You will land on the following screen where you associate an S3 bucket for the server to store the pipeline definition files and related artifacts. Use the following settings:

```
Name: wines
AWS_ACCESS_KEY_ID: minio
AWS_SECRET_ACCESS_KEY: minio123
AWS_S3_ENDPOINT: http://minio-ml-workshop.minio.svc.cluster.
local:9000
AWS_S3_BUCKET: pipelines
```

Make sure that the MinIO location is mentioned correctly. Click on the **Configure** button so that OpenShift will provision a pipeline server for your data science project:

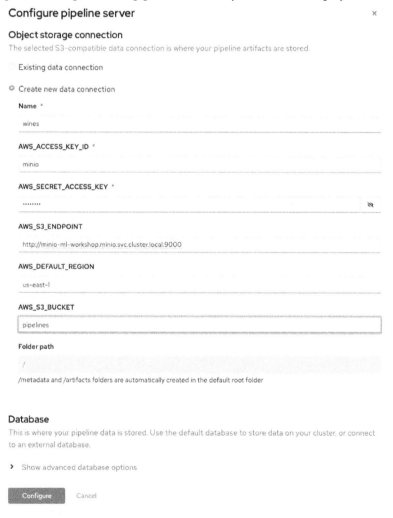

Figure 4.13 – Creating a pipeline server

You have successfully created a pipeline server. Now, let's build and deploy a basic data science pipeline.

Building a basic data science pipeline

In the previous section, you created a notebook to train your model. Using OpenShift Pipelines, you will define an end-to-end ML and data workflow that includes a model training job. In this section, you will start with a basic pipeline and continue building it in the remaining part of this book. You will be using the **Elyra JupyterLab** extension to create and run data science pipelines within a Jupyter notebook using drag-and-drop capabilities. Each stage of a pipeline will be executed by a container in OpenShift, and you will control the execution process through the Jupyter notebook.

Follow these steps to build your first data science pipeline:

1. Start by loading **Pipeline Editor** from the launcher page as shown in *Figure 4.14*, under the **Elyra** heading:

Figure 4.14 – Creating an Elyra pipeline

2. You will see the screen shown in *Figure 4.15*. Drag and drop the `wine-training.ipynb` file into the workspace:

Figure 4.15 – Creating a pipeline via Elyra

3. Open the properties panel on the right side and select the container image that will run this stage of your pipeline. Select the image named **Datascience with Python 3.9**, as shown in *Figure 4.15*. This is the same image that you have chosen for the notebook so that the runtime environment remains consistent.

4. Save your pipeline as `wines.pipeline` in the notebook. Then, click on the **Runtimes** button on the left pane to validate the pipeline configuration. *Figure 4.16* shows the runtime configuration. Note that the location of **Cloud Object Storage** has the configuration that you set for your pipelines in the earlier section:

Figure 4.16 – Creating a pipeline via Elyra

5. Now, open the `wines.pipeline` file and click on the **Export Pipeline** icon on the top toolbar. This will generate the pipeline code and upload the associated files, such as the notebook, to the `pipelines` S3 bucket. You will see in *Figure 4.17* that the first drop-down box is the name of the runtime and the second drop-down box is the format of the file, which can be either *YAML* or *Python*. Select the YAML format, enter the name of the file, and hit **OK**:

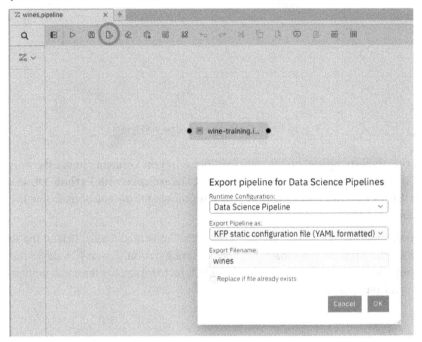

Figure 4.17 – Exporting the pipeline

Apart from uploading the pipelines' artifacts to the `pipelines` S3 bucket, a `wines.yaml` file is also created in the workspace. Download the file and navigate to the Red Hat data science dashboard where you will upload this pipeline YAML file.

6. Open your Red Hat ODS project and click on the **Import pipeline** button. You will see a screen like the one shown in *Figure 4.18*. Name the pipeline `wines` and upload the `wines.yaml` file via the **Upload** button:

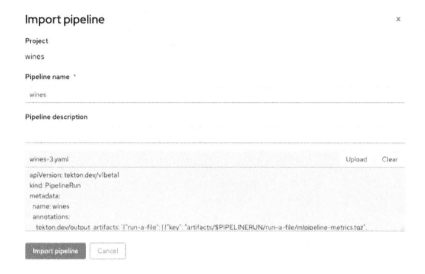

Figure 4.18 – Importing pipeline to OpenShift

7. Click **Import pipeline**, and you will have a pipeline displayed in the data science dashboard, as shown in *Figure 4.19*:

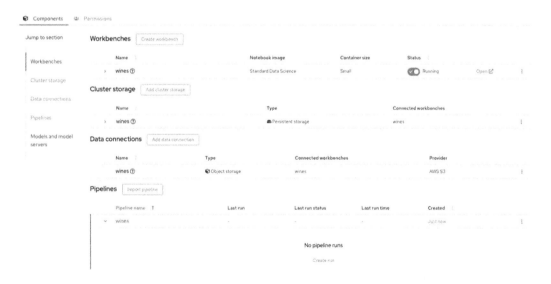

Figure 4.19 – Data science project dashboard showing wines pipeline

8. Now, you can schedule the pipeline execution by clicking on the **Create run** link under your `wines` pipeline. You will see a page like the one shown in *Figure 4.20*. Here, you can name your run and define **Run type** as either run on demand or on a schedule:

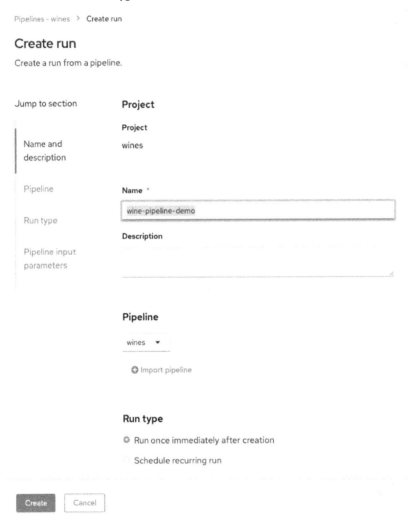

Figure 4.20 – Running OpenShift pipeline

9. Click on the **Create** button, and OpenShift will schedule your pipeline for execution. You will see a screen visualizing the status of your pipeline run, as shown in *Figure 4.21*:

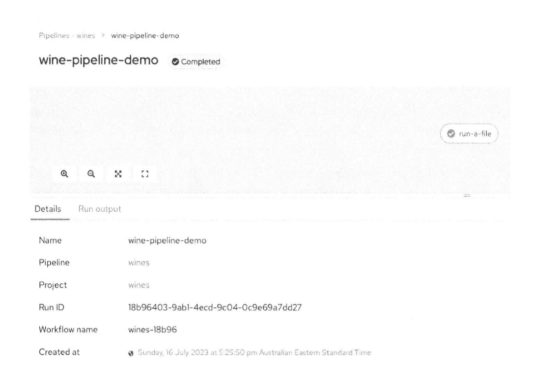

Figure 4.21 – OpenShift pipeline execution

You can see the full execution logs of the pipelines from the OpenShift data science dashboard by going to the **Data Science Pipelines** -> **Runs** menu on the left pane. A sample of the screen is shown in *Figure 4.22*:

Figure 4.22 – OpenShift pipeline history

You have just successfully built, deployed, and executed a simple model training pipeline using ODS. Notice how easy it is to build pipelines using Elyra's drag-and-drop capability and run the notebook that you have used for the development. The consistency, ease of use, and automation capability provided by the platform will definitely improve your data team's velocity.

Summary

In this chapter, you have seen how Red Hat ODS integrates with third-party software to further simplify your MLOps journey. OpenShift makes it a breeze to use the data versioning capabilities of the Pachyderm software.

You have seen how Red Hat OpenShift Pipelines enables your data science team to automate the model training workflow by providing drag-and-drop capabilities and using the same code you have used to manually train the model.

You will use the core pipeline capabilities in the next few chapters, where you'll further automate your workflow. In the next chapter, you will use what you have learned about creating pipelines to deploy the model as a service.

5

Deploying ML Models as a Service

In the previous chapter, you built a model using RHODS. In this chapter, you will start packaging and deploying your models as a service. You will see that you do not need any application development experience to expose your model. This capability enables your data science teams to be more agile in testing new models and making them available for consumption.

In this chapter, we will cover the following topics.

- Packaging and deploying models as a service
- Autoscaling the deployed models
- Releasing new versions of the model
- Securing the deployed model endpoint

Before we start, please make sure that you have completed the model-building steps and performed the configuration mentioned in the previous chapter. We'll start by exposing our model as an HTTP service.

Packaging and deploying models as a service

To take advantage of the scalability of OpenShift workloads, the best way to run inferences against an ML model is to deploy the model as an HTTP service. This way, inference calls can be performed by invoking the HTTP endpoint of a model server Pod that is running the model. You can then create multiple replicas of the model server, allowing you to horizontally scale your model to serve more requests.

Recall that you built the wine quality prediction model in the previous chapter. The first stage of exposing the model is to save your model in an S3 bucket. RHODS provides multiple model servers that host your models and allow them to be accessed over HTTP. Think of it as an application server such as JBoss or WebLogic, which takes your Java code and enables it to be executed and accessed over standard protocols.

The model servers can serve different types of model formats, such as *Intel OpenVINO*, which uses the **Open Neural Network Exchange Format** (**ONXX**). This format represents many types of ML frameworks, such as *PyTorch* and *TensorFlow*. You can also create custom servers to support the format that you use.

We'll start by saving our model using the *scikit Joblib* format, after which we'll define a Seldon-based model server to host our model. Don't worry – it is much easier than it sounds thanks to OpenShift.

Saving and uploading models to S3

Before we start, create a bucket named `wine-models` in the *MinIO* server. This bucket is where you will upload the models. Open the `chapter5/wine-training-model.ipynb` file, which is similar to the file you used in the previous chapter. The only difference is that you are saving the model as a *Joblib* file in the cell, as shown here:

```
# Save the model to a file
with open('model.joblib', 'wb') as f:
pickle.dump(wine_ln_reg, f)
```

Next, upload the saved model to the newly created bucket. Open the `chapter5/upload-model.ipynb` file; this will upload the model to the **wine-models** bucket. The code uses the *boto3* library, a Python S3 object storage client, to upload the file to the S3 bucket. If your notebook environment does not have boto3 installed, you can install it by adding the following line of code in a cell of your notebook:

```
!pip install boto3

# Set up the S3 client
s3 = boto3.client('s3',
endpoint_url='http://minio-ml-workshop.minio.svc.cluster.local:9000',
aws_access_key_id='minio',
aws_secret_access_key=os.getenv("MODEL_REGISTRY_PASSWORD"))

# Upload a file to the bucket
bucket_name = 'wine-models'
object_name = 'models/model.joblib'
file_path = 'model.joblib'

s3.upload_file(file_path, bucket_name, object_name)
```

You may have noticed that the password has been injected from an environment variable, which is made available from the environment variable settings of your workbench, as shown in *Figure 5.1*:

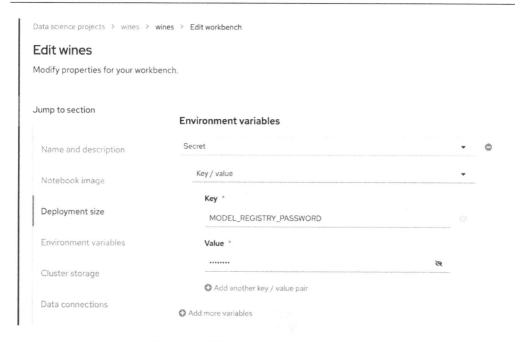

Figure 5.1 – Workbench environment variables

Now that our code is complete, let's update the pipeline so that it trains and uploads the model in two stages.

Updating the pipeline via model upload to S3

In the previous chapter, you created a pipeline that runs your notebook to train the wine quality model. In this section, you will enhance the pipeline with two stages – one to build and save the model and another to upload it. You will also see how the data flows between two stages – for example, how the model built in the first stage of your pipeline needs to be shared with the second stage so that it can be uploaded. Let's begin:

1. Start by creating a pipeline named `wine-train-upload` in the notebook environment.

2. Drag and drop the two files, `chapter5/wine-training-model.ipynb` and `chapter5/upload-model.ipynb`, and connect them, as shown in *Figure 5.2*. You can connect them by clicking on the first node and connecting it to the second node:

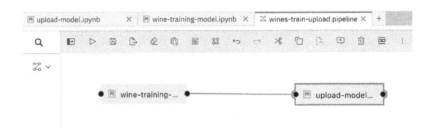

Figure 5.2 – Pipeline showing connected notebook jobs

3. Associate the correct **runtime image** with each of these nodes. For this example, set **Datascience with Python 3.9 (UBI9)**, as you did in the previous chapter.

4. Now, we need to tell the pipeline that the first node will create a file called `model.joblib`, which is required by the second node. Click on the first node, open the **Properties** panel on the right, and add the file to the **Output Files** section, as shown in *Figure 5.3*. The Red Hat pipelines will make sure that the file is available to all the remaining nodes in the pipeline.

Figure 5.3 – The pipeline job's output file configuration

5. Open the **Properties** panel for the second node; you will find that the pipeline automatically detects the environment variables that your code is using. Recall that the code is using the `MODEL_REGISTRY_PASSWORD` variable; this is shown in the **Properties** panel for the node. For the production system, you will use Kubernetes Secrets integration, which is provided out of the box. Here, you can mention the secret name on the same screen; see the bottom part of *Figure 5.4*. However, for simplicity, we have added the value as an environment variable. You should always use Kubernetes Secrets, even in lower environments:

Figure 5.4 – Pipeline job environment variables configuration

6. Save the pipeline, export it, and register and run it in RHODS. Refer to the previous chapter on exporting and importing the pipeline for more details. Name the new pipeline `wine-train-upload`. Then, create an on-demand run named `wine-train-upload-run`. Once it's been executed, it will look as follows:

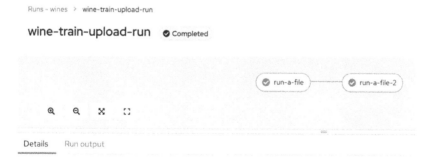

Figure 5.5 – Successful pipeline run

7. Validate that the file has been uploaded to the **wine-models** bucket.

Now that you have uploaded the model to S3, you'll learn how to configure the model server and expose your uploaded model as a service.

Creating a model server for Seldon

We have chosen *SeldonIO* as the model server because it is open source and provides capabilities to host *Joblib* models. Seldon Core is available under an Apache 2.0 license. Combining it with containers and the power of OpenShift, you can scale to serve thousands of concurrent requests. Let's take a look:

1. Open RHODS and click on the **Serving runtimes** link in the **Settings** menu item. You will see the following screen, which contains the pre-packaged model servers:

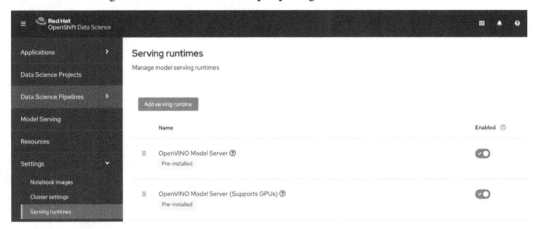

Figure 5.6 – Serving runtimes

2. Click on the **Add serving runtime** button and upload the `chapter5/custom-runtime.yaml` file. Your model server will be registered, as shown here:

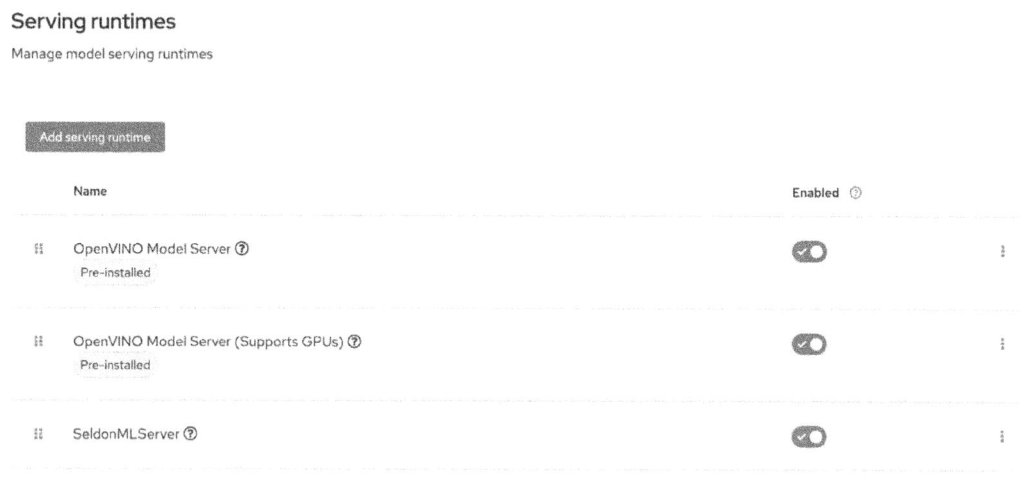

Serving runtimes

Manage model serving runtimes

Figure 5.7 – Successfully adding a custom model serving runtime

You have just created a custom model serving runtime in your RHODS platform. Now, let's understand the important parts of the custom runtime's YAML manifest file. The first part is the list of supported formats that your server can provide. This list will be made available later to the model deployment team. Since Seldon supports these three formats, among others, we have provided them as a list:

```
supportedModelFormats:
- name: sklearn
  version: "0" # v0.23.1
  autoSelect: true
- name: xgboost
  version: "1" # v1.1.1
  autoSelect: true
- name: lightgbm
  version: "3" # v3.2.1
  autoSelect: true
```

Then, you must provide the container image location of the Seldon server:

```
containers:
- name: mlserver
  image: seldonio/mlserver:0.5.2
```

You can also provide the resource requirements and limits for your server, just like you would for a regular Kubernetes Deployment resource:

> **Note**
>
> Notice that one server can serve multiple models, so you will be able to adjust it accordingly when you are registering it later in this chapter.

```
resources:
requests:
cpu: 500m
memory: 1Gi
limits:
cpu: "5"
memory: 1Gi
```

Next, you must deploy the model that you uploaded to S3 in the previous section.

Deploying and accessing your model

You'll start by registering the model server using the runtime you created in the previous stage within your workspace:

1. Go to the **wines** data science project and, under the **Models and model servers** link within your project, click **Add Server**. You should see the **Add model server** screen, as shown in *Figure 5.8*.

2. Select the **SeldonMLServer** runtime, give it a name of your choice, such as wine, and select **Small** for **Model server size**. Finally, click **Add** to register your server. Note that the checkbox for **Model route** is ticked; this means that OpenShift will make your model available to the consumers outside the cluster. You can also choose to expose your model to internal applications only, depending on your needs:

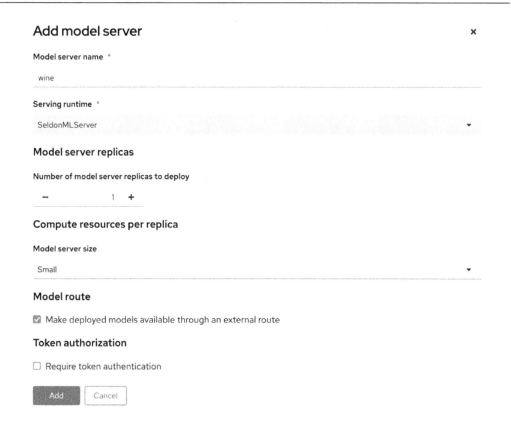

Figure 5.8 – The Add model server screen

3. Now, it's time to deploy the model. Click on the **Deploy model** button that appears next to your registered server in your workspace, as shown in *Figure 5.9*:

Figure 5.9 – RHODS showing models and model servers

4. You will see the screen shown in *Figure 5.10*; this is where you provide details of the model to be deployed. Here, you must define **Model framework**; this is **sklearn - 0** in our case. In this dropdown, you will see the list of supported models that we defined while configuring the **Seldon** model serving runtime. So, the platform team will define the runtime and associated configuration and the data science team will use this screen to deploy. You must also define the S3 connection to load the models from. This is the same taxonomy that you used previously and you can either create a new data connection for your **wine-models** bucket or use an existing one if you have one. The data science team does not need to understand the application-level details to expose the model. Once you've done this, hit **Deploy**; your model will be deployed and accessible over an HTTP connection:

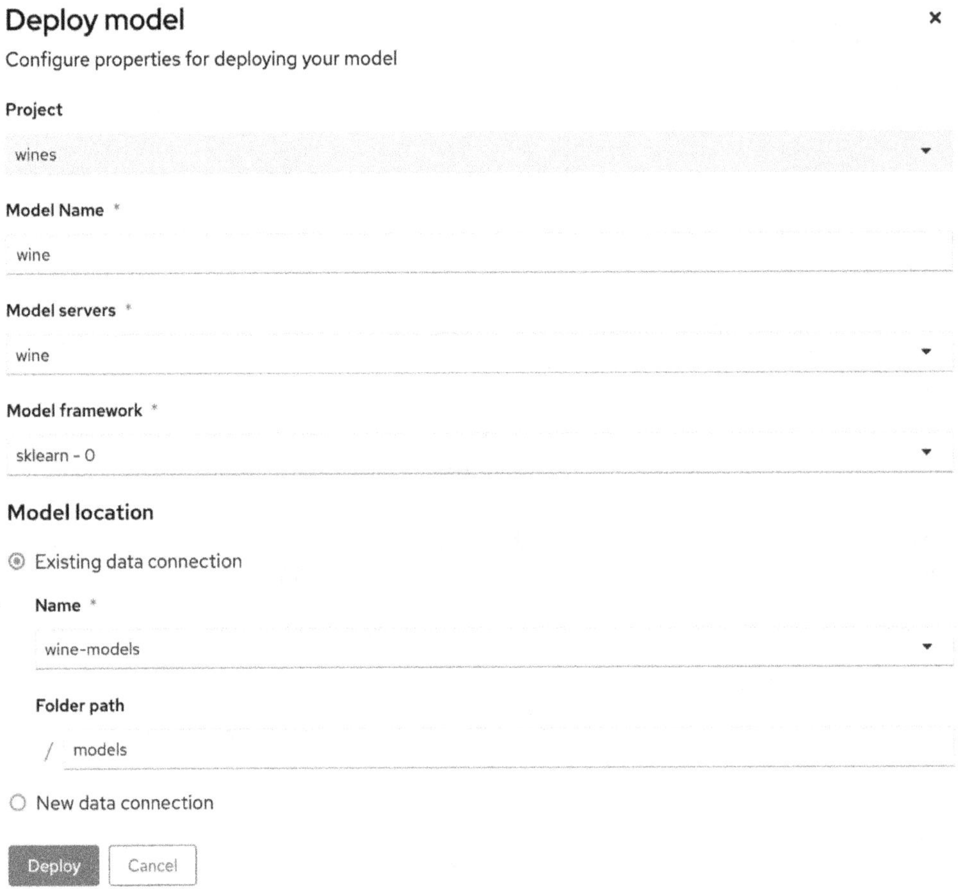

Deploy model   ✕

Configure properties for deploying your model

Project

wines   ▾

Model Name *

wine

Model servers *

wine   ▾

Model framework *

sklearn - 0   ▾

Model location

◉ Existing data connection

   Name *

   wine-models   ▾

   Folder path

   /   models

○ New data connection

[Deploy] [Cancel]

Figure 5.10 – The Deploy model dialog

5. Congratulations! Your model has been deployed and is available for users to use. You will see the model's URL in the **Inference endpoint** section, as shown in *Figure 5.11*:

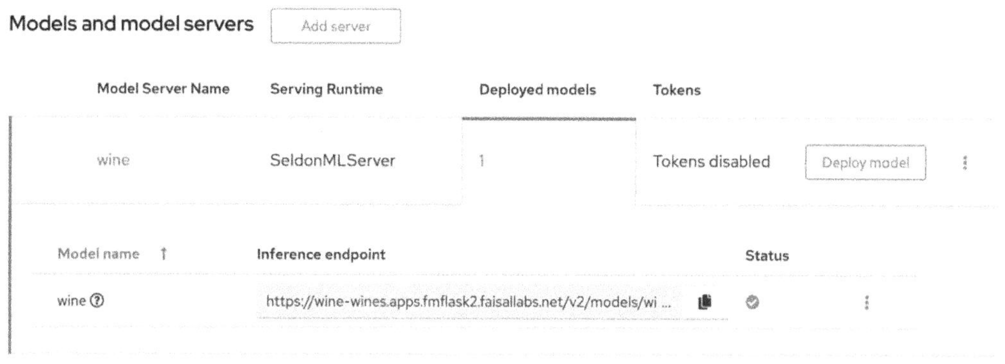

Models and model servers   Add server

Model Server Name	Serving Runtime	Deployed models	Tokens
wine	SeldonMLServer	1	Tokens disabled Deploy model ⋮

Model name ↑	Inference endpoint		Status
wine ⑦	https://wine-wines.apps.fmflask2.faisallabs.net/v2/models/wi ... 📋		⊘ ⋮

Figure 5.11 – The Models and model servers screen showing the deployed model

Now that you have deployed your model to OpenShift and exposed it as an HTTP server, the next step is to write some code so that you can perform inferencing against the model. This is the code that the consumers of your model will write. You can find this code in the `chapter5/call-model.ipynb` file. Let's see the basic part of the code.

You must start by defining your payload. For this, you must define the columns you used to train the model. Based on this data, it will predict the quality of the wine:

```
data = {'volatile acidity': [0.17],
'residual sugar': [1.5],
'chlorides': [0.032],
'total sulfur dioxide': [112.0],
'sulphates': [0.55],
'alcohol': [11.4]
}
```

Then, create a pandas DataFrame from `data` and call it `wine_0`, as shown in the following line of code:

```
wine_0 = pd.DataFrame(data)
```

Next, create the payload for your inference request. This payload is expected by your inference server, which is Seldon in our case:

```
inference_request = {
"inputs": [
{
"name": "predict",
"shape": wine_0.shape,
"datatype": "FP32",
"data": wine_0.loc[:].values.tolist()
}
]
}
```

Then, simply make the HTTP call to the inference endpoint. This will print out the response, which contains details of the wine's quality:

```
endpoint = "https://wine-wines.apps.fmflask2.faisallabs.net/v2/models/
wine/infer"
response = requests.post(endpoint, json=inference_request,
verify=False)


response.json()
```

The output will look as follows, with the data field containing the wine's quality. This output is a response from the Seldon server. Different runtimes may have different output formats:

```
{'model_name': 'wine__isvc-12fe7f5899', \
    'outputs': [{'name': 'predict', 'datatype': 'FP64', \
    'shape': [1], 'data': [6.324527141615349]}]}
```

Your model is now working hard for your consumers. While the number of inference calls to your model increases, the required compute resources also increase. In such cases, you will need to increase the number of running instances of your model server to distribute the load across multiple model server instances. By taking advantage of OpenShift's autoscaling feature, you can automate the scaling of your model server instances depending on the load.

Now, let's see how easy it is to configure the autoscaling of your model server.

Autoscaling the deployed models

While creating a model server, you will be presented with the option to set the number of replicas. This corresponds to the number of instances of the model servers to be created. This allows you to increase or decrease the serving capacity of your model servers. *Figure 5.12* shows this option as **Model server replicas**:

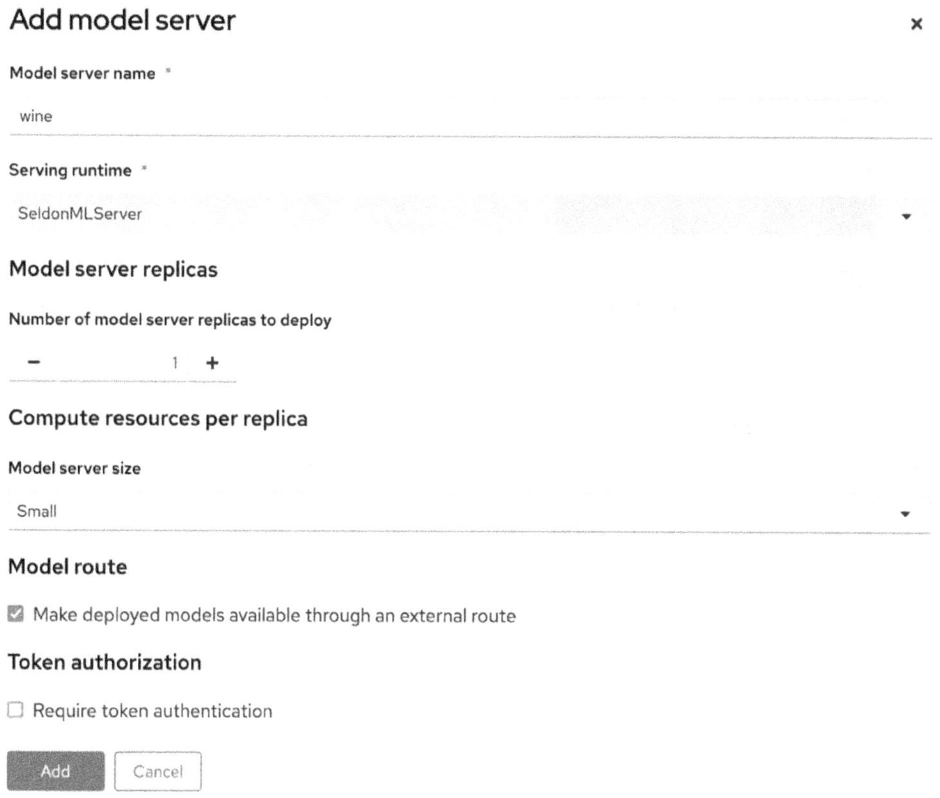

Add model server   ✕

Model server name *

wine

Serving runtime *

SeldonMLServer   ▾

Model server replicas

Number of model server replicas to deploy

−   1   +

Compute resources per replica

Model server size

Small   ▾

Model route

☑ Make deployed models available through an external route

Token authorization

☐ Require token authentication

[Add]   [Cancel]

Figure 5.12 – Add model server

However, with this approach, you need to decide on the number of serving instances or replicas at the time of the model server's creation. OpenShift provides another construct where you can add an automatic scaler that increases or decreases the number of replicas of the model server based on the memory or CPU utilization of the model server instances. This construct is called **horizontal pod autoscaling**. This allows us to automatically scale workloads to match the demand.

Let's see how the model server that we defined with the data science project is deployed. First, your **wines** data science project was created as an OpenShift project. Go to the OpenShift console and find the **wines** project, as shown in *Figure 5.13*:

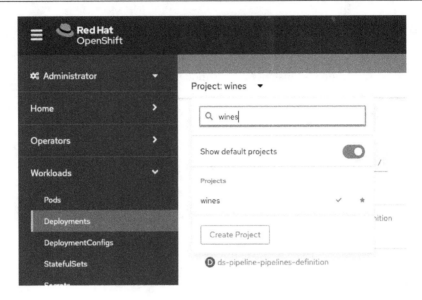

Figure 5.13 – Deployments

Now, navigate to the **Deployments** option from the left menu; you will find a deployment option named **modelmesh-serving-wine**, where **wine** is the name of your model server. Notice that it has one pod. Now, go to your data science project and click on the three dots on the right-hand side of your model server, as shown in *Figure 5.14*:

Figure 5.14 – Edit model server

Click on **Edit model server** and increase the number of replicas to **2** in the popup that appears, as shown in *Figure 5.15*:

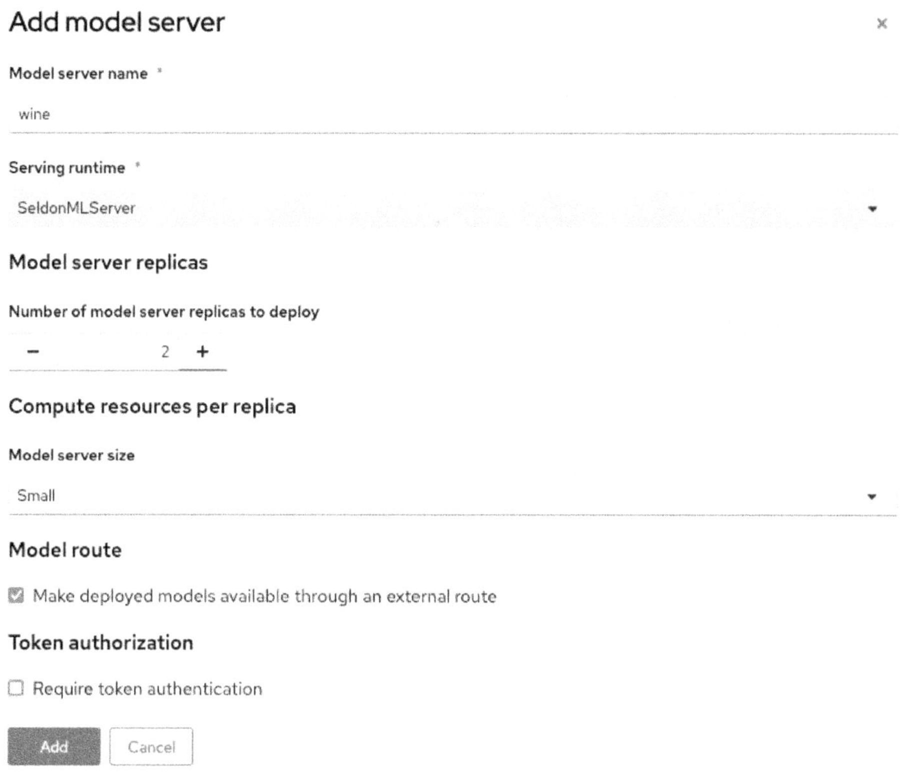

Add model server   ✕

Model server name *

wine

Serving runtime *

SeldonMLServer   ▾

Model server replicas

Number of model server replicas to deploy

—   2   +

Compute resources per replica

Model server size

Small   ▾

Model route

☑ Make deployed models available through an external route

Token authorization

☐ Require token authentication

Add   Cancel

Figure 5.15 – Editing the number of model replicas to deploy

Save this and go to the OpenShift console. Here, select the **wines** project, then **Deployments**. You will see that the **modelmesh-serving-wine** deployment now has two replicas, as shown in *Figure 5.16*:

Figure 5.16 – The model serving deployment resource showing two replicas

Now that you have seen that editing the number of model server replicas just involves changing the number of replicas of the associated deployment resource, change the number of replicas of your model server back to **1**; we will show you how to automate this process next.

To add automatic scaling to the deployment, click on the **modelmesh-serving-wine** deployment in the OpenShift console, then click on the **Actions** drop-down menu on the far right, as shown in *Figure 5.17*:

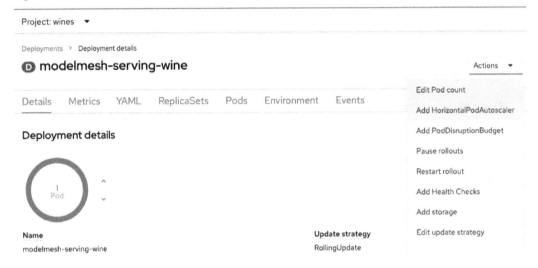

Figure 5.17 – Deployment details

Click the **Add HorizontalPodAutoscaler** option; you will be presented with the screen shown in *Figure 5.18*. Start by giving your autoscaler a name, such as `wine-model-server-autoscaler`. Next, provide the minimum and maximum number of pods since you do not want it to scale indefinitely. Then, provide a threshold in terms of the percentage of CPU and memory utilization. When the model server hits this threshold, OpenShift will automatically add a new Pod. OpenShift will reduce the number of Pods to a minimum if the Pods are not busy as per the provided threshold. This is how a fully elastic model server will be managed by RHODS for you. The **Add HorizontalPodAutoscaler** screen is shown in *Figure 5.18*:

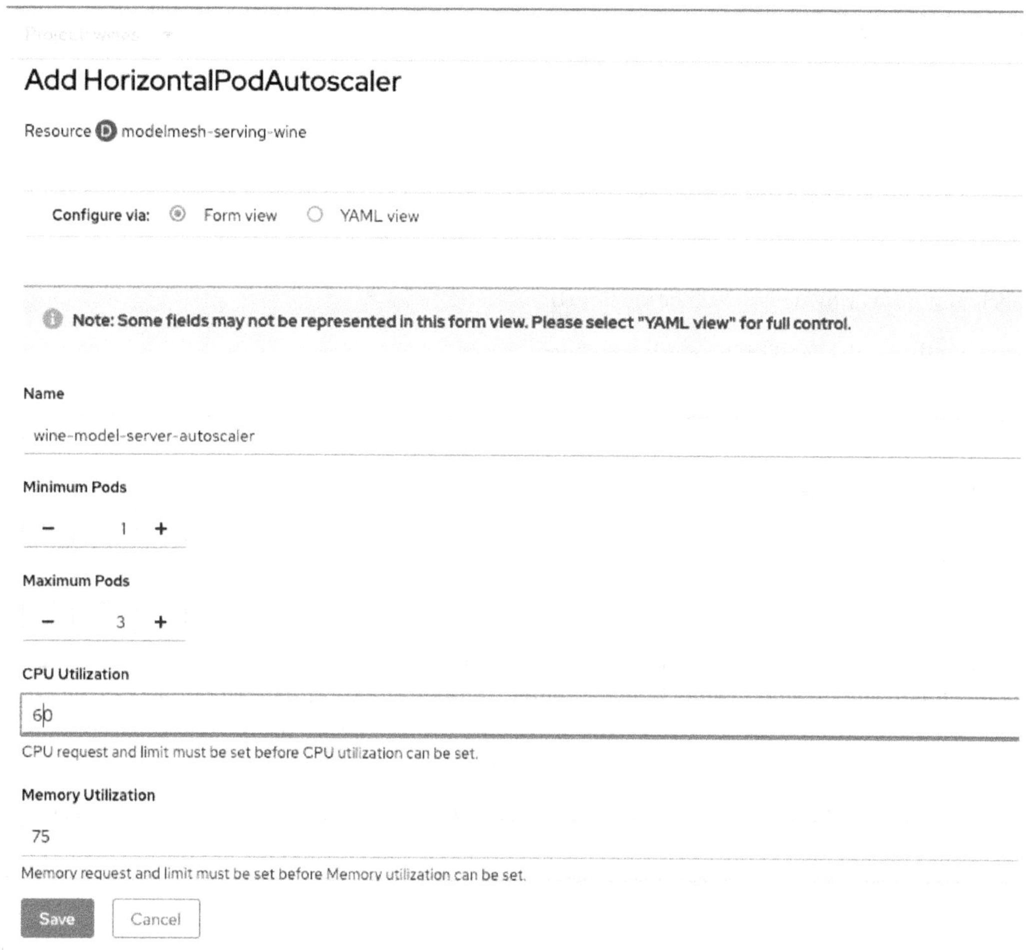

Add HorizontalPodAutoscaler

Resource Ⓓ modelmesh-serving-wine

Configure via: ⦿ Form view   ◯ YAML view

ⓘ **Note: Some fields may not be represented in this form view. Please select "YAML view" for full control.**

Name

wine-model-server-autoscaler

Minimum Pods

— 1 +

Maximum Pods

— 3 +

CPU Utilization

60

CPU request and limit must be set before CPU utilization can be set.

Memory Utilization

75

Memory request and limit must be set before Memory utilization can be set.

Save   Cancel

Figure 5.18 – Add HorizontalPodAutoscaler

RHODS makes it extremely easy to automatically scale your model server. Now, when the load increases, OpenShift will create a new pod and reduce the number of pods to the minimum value during quieter times.

Next, you'll learn how to release a newer version of the model.

Releasing new versions of the model

Having a model served as a service is not the end of the story. For the model to stay relevant and continue to deliver value to the business, you will need to keep it updated. You will continually release new versions of the model to keep up with the changing environment and to address model drift. Additionally, releasing a new version of the model may fail, and/or the new models may not perform as expected. In such cases, you may want to redeploy a newer version or roll back to the previous version of the model to avoid service disruptions. This is why it is important to not overwrite existing models and this is why they should be versioned.

To version the model, we'll create a new pipeline:

1. In the **wines** workbench, open a new pipeline editor by going to **File | New | Data Science Pipeline Editor**.

2. Drag and drop the `wine-training-model.ipynb` and the `upload-model-versioned.ipynb` notebook files into the workspace. This will create jobs in the pipeline that will execute all cells in the notebook file. The `upload-model-versioned.ipynb` notebook file is similar to the original `upload-model.ipynb` notebook file but with minor differences in the model upload process. In this new notebook, instead of replacing the existing model in the **model registry**, we are creating another copy of the model by appending the model version in the model directory name. In this example, the model version is derived from the current date and time. You may also use other versioning strategies, such as the traditional series of integers in the format of *major.minor.build* or using a Git *commit hash*.

3. Connect the two jobs, starting with **wine-training-job**. Your workspace should look what's shown in *Figure 5.19*:

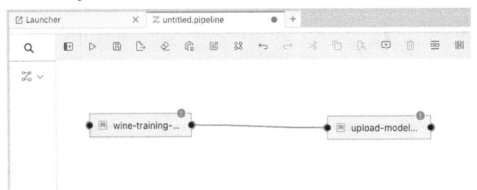

Figure 5.19 – Pipeline editor showing the new pipeline

4. Configure **wine-training-job** by right-clicking the box and selecting **Open Properties**. In the **Properties** pane, set the runtime image to **Datascience with Python 3.9 (UBI9)**, as shown in *Figure 5.20*.

5. Because the wine training job will produce the `model.joblib` model file, we need to declare the model file as the output of this job so that the succeeding job can access it. Click the **Add** button under the **Output Files** section of the **Properties** pane. Set the filename to `model.joblib`, as shown in *Figure 5.20*. This will allow the succeeding jobs to access the model file:

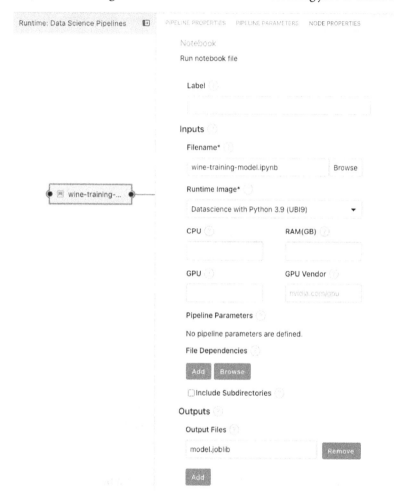

Figure 5.20 – Properties of wine-training-job

6. Set the properties of the **upload-model-versioned** job and set the runtime image to **Datascience with Python 3.9 (UBI9)**, as shown in *Figure 5.21*.

7. On the same **Properties** pane, create an output file called `vars.txt` and set the `MODEL_REGISTRY_PASSWORD` variable to `minio123`, as shown in *Figure 5.21*. This is the password of the S3 server that we are using as model file storage. The `vars.txt` file is used to pass variables to the succeeding jobs – in this case, the model version:

Figure 5.21 – Properties of upload-model-versioned

8. Save the pipeline and then export it to a file named `versioned-model-training-pipeline.yaml`, as shown in *Figure 5.22*. This will create a new file in the workspace:

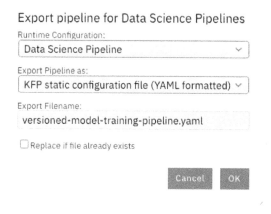

Figure 5.22 – Export pipeline for Data Science Pipelines

9. Now, let's import this pipeline's *YAML* file into our RHODS workspace. Download the file from the workbench onto your local machine. On the RHODS data science project page, click the **Import pipeline** button.

10. In the **Import pipeline** dialog, set the name of the pipeline, as shown in *Figure 5.22*, then click the **Import pipeline** button:

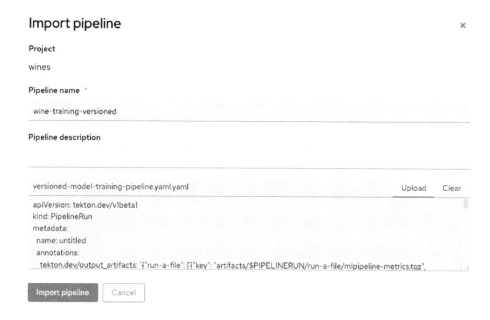

Figure 5.23 – The Import pipeline dialog for the versioned pipeline

After importing the pipeline successfully, it should be listed in the **Pipeline** section of your data science project page.

11. Now, let's run the pipeline manually. Select the **wine-training-versioned** pipeline and click the **Create run** link. You should see a page similar to the one shown in *Figure 5.24*:

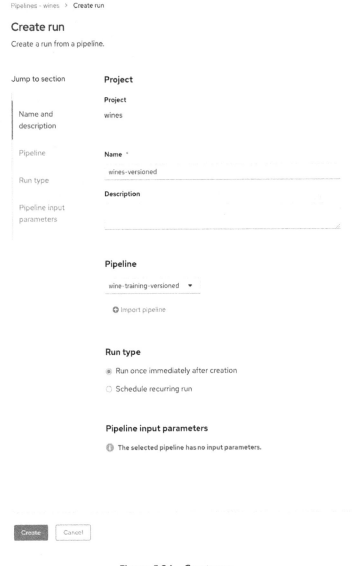

Figure 5.24 – Create run

12. Set the pipeline run options to their defaults, as shown in *Figure 5.24*, and click the **Create** button. This will create a new *PipelineRun* object in OpenShift and will immediately start executing.

13. Wait for the pipeline to complete successfully. Navigate to your *MinIO* page and browse the **wine-models** bucket. You should see a new directory named *model-\<version-number\>*, as shown in *Figure 5.25*. The version number will be different in your environment:

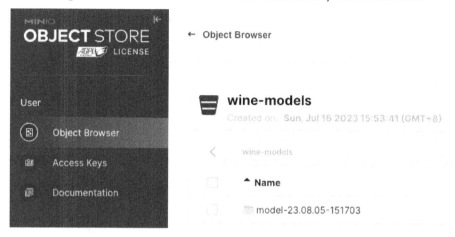

Figure 5.25 – The MinIO browser showing the versioned model

14. Create another pipeline run or duplicate the pipeline run and observe the bucket in the *MinIO* object browser. You will observe that every time this pipeline runs, a new versioned copy of the model is uploaded to the bucket.

> **Note**
>
> For larger models, such as deep neural networks, you may want to use a proper **model registry** such as **MLflow**. Model registries act both as model storage and model version control.

You have just created and executed a model training pipeline that uploads a versioned copy of the model every time it is executed. Now, let's learn how to automatically deploy models to our model server.

Automating the model deployment process

To complete the pipeline, we want it to include a step that will automatically deploy the new version of the model to the model server. When you manually deployed a model previously, behind the scenes, you created a new OpenShift custom resource called `InferenceService`. Automating the deployment of a new model means automating the update or creation of the *InferenceService* resource. *InferenceService* is a custom resource that comes with RHODS. By adding this custom resource to your OpenShift cluster, a model deployment is created in RHODS. This means you can create model deployments that are deployed to your model servers by creating custom *InferenceService* resources without going through the web console.

In this book's GitHub repository, there is a notebook file called `deploy-model.ipynb`. We will use this notebook to deploy models automatically to our OpenShift cluster. Let's have a quick look at what this notebook does.

First, we must retrieve the necessary variables from `vars.txt`. The version number of the model is retrieved from this file:

```
variables = {}
with open("vars.txt") as myfile:
    for line in myfile:
        name, var = line.partition("=")[::2]
        variables[name.strip()] = str(var)
```

The second part makes use of the `inference-service.yaml` file as the manifest file for creating or updating the custom *InferenceService* OpenShift resource. The following code updates the YAML file by replacing all `{{ model_version }}` text with the actual model version to be deployed:

```
template_data = {"model_version": variables['model_version']}
template = Template(open("inference-service.yaml").read())
rendered_template = template.render(template_data)
print('Rendered Template: \r' + rendered_template)
```

The final part of the code uses the **OpenShift Client** (`oc`) command to apply the rendered *YAML* text to the OpenShift cluster:

```
subprocess.run(['oc', 'whoami'])
ps = subprocess.Popen(['echo', rendered_template], \
    stdout=subprocess.PIPE)
output = subprocess.check_output(['oc', 'apply', '-f', '-'], \
    stdin=ps.stdout)
ps.wait()
print(output)
print('Model deployment completed. Version: ' + variables['model_
version'])
```

The preceding code is the Python equivalent of running the following shell command:

```
echo <the rendered yaml string> | oc apply -f-
```

Now, let's add this notebook to our pipeline to complete the pipeline workflow.

Follow these steps to add this notebook to the pipeline:

1. Open the pipeline file that you created in the previous section.
2. Drag and drop the `deploy-model.ipynb` notebook file into the pipeline editor workspace.

3. Connect the **upload-model-versioned** job to this new job, as shown in *Figure 5.26*, and set the runtime image to **Datascience with Python 3.9 (UBI9)**.

4. Add a file dependency to `inference-service.yaml`, as shown in *Figure 5.26*:

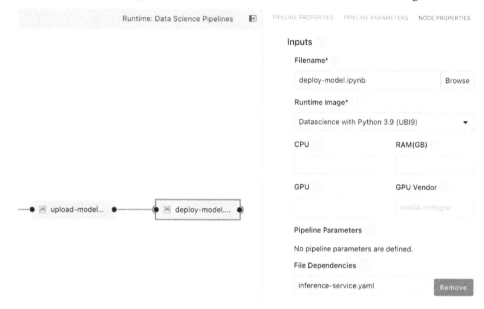

Figure 5.26 – The deploy-model job's properties

5. Now, save the pipeline file and export it as a *KFP* pipeline file called `full-pipeline`, as shown in *Figure 5.27*. This will generate the pipeline's YAML file in the workspace:

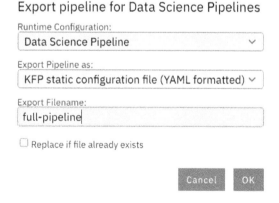

Figure 5.27 – Export pipeline for Data Science Pipelines

6. Upload the generated YAML file to your data science workspace and name it `full-pipeline`, as shown in *Figure 5.28*:

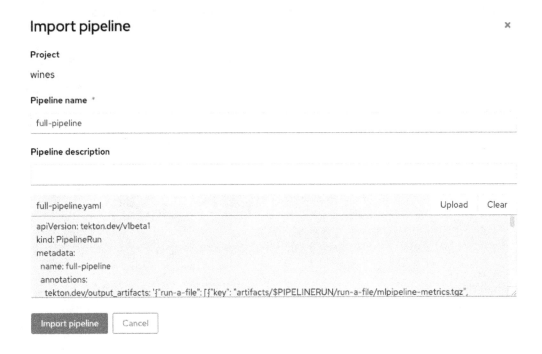

Figure 5.28 – Import pipeline

7. The imported pipeline will be listed as a new pipeline in your data science workspace, where you can create a pipeline run. Click the **Create run** link to create an on-demand *PipelineRun* resource, as shown in *Figure 5.29*:

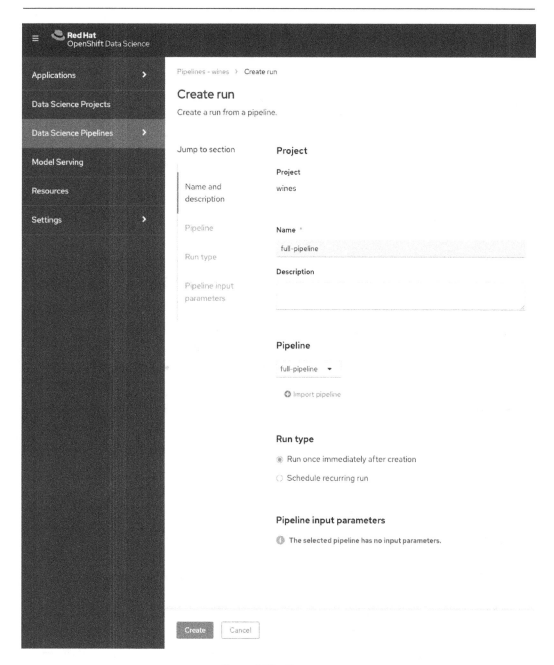

Figure 5.29 – Create run

8. Click the **Create** button to create the run. The *PipelineRun* will start executing immediately after being created. Wait for the pipeline to complete. It will look like what's shown in *Figure 5.30*, showing all the jobs with a green tick:

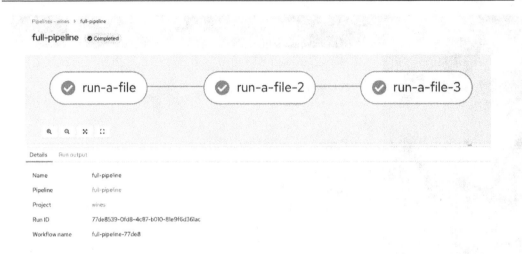

Figure 5.30 – The pipeline run was completed successfully

9. Now, let's verify whether the pipeline has deployed a new version of the model. To do this, navigate to the **Models and model servers** section of your data science project page. In the **Deployed models** column, you should see more two models under the **wine** model server. The model name also contains the version number of the model that was deployed by the pipeline, as shown in *Figure 5.31*:

Figure 5.31 – New model name under the wine model server

10. Verify the deployment by using the `call-model.ipynb` notebook. Change the endpoint URL to the URL of your new model and run it.

11. Re-run the pipeline by duplicating the *PipelineRun* and observe how the version number changes. You can find the **Duplicate run** button on the pipeline run page, as shown in *Figure 5.32*:

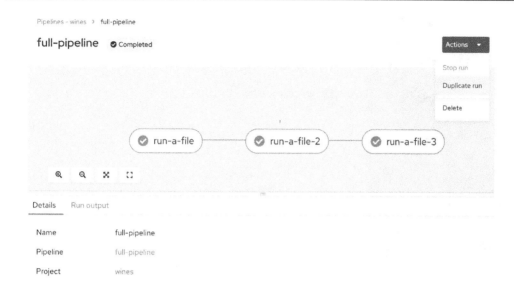

Figure 5.32 – Duplicate run

12. Notice that in the **Models and model servers** section, the name of the model has changed and has a different version number.

Congratulations! You have just created a complete data science pipeline that automatically trains a model, uploads a model to model storage, and deploys it automatically to your model servers. We've also prepared the `full-pipeline.pipeline` file in the Git repository for your reference.

In the next section, we will learn how to roll back a deployment to an earlier version.

Rolling back model deployments

There are instances where a rollback is necessary for many reasons. This could be because the new release has failed to perform as expected or for any other reasons. Nevertheless, the ability to roll back a model deployment is an essential part of any **MLOps** strategy.

The simplest way to roll back a deployment is to deploy an earlier version of the deployment artifact, which in this case is the model. Because we have created versioned copies of our models for each training pipeline run, this means that we have copies of all the versions of our model in our model storage or registry. If you navigate to the *MinIO* object browser, then the **wine-models** bucket, you will see multiple folders containing different versions of our model, similar to what's shown in *Figure 5.33*:

Figure 5.33 – The MinIO object browser showing model versions

In this book's GitHub repository, under the `chapter5` folder, there is a notebook file named `deploy-model-version.ipynb`. This notebook is a modified version of the `deploy-model.ipynb` notebook file. The only difference is that this notebook gets the model version from an environment variable instead of getting it from the previous jobs in the pipeline. This means that this notebook can deploy any model versions, so long as they exist in the **model registry**.

Let's have a look at how to use the `deploy-model-version.ipynb` notebook to implement a pipeline that can perform a model deployment rollback. The following steps will guide you through this process:

1. Open a new Elyra pipeline editor window.

2. Drag and drop the `deploy-model-version.ipynb` notebook file into the pipeline editor workspace.

3. Create a new pipeline parameter by opening the **Properties** pane and selecting the **Pipeline Parameters** tab.

4. Create a new pipeline parameter by clicking the **Add** button. Provide the values shown in *Figure 5.34*:

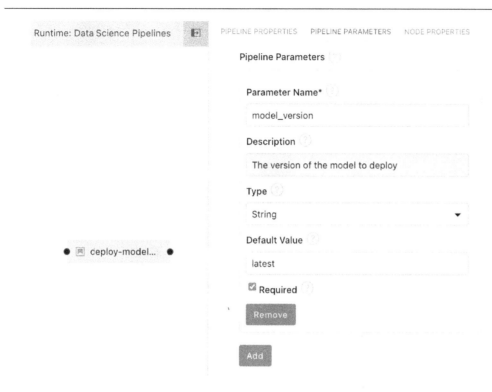

Figure 5.34 – Elyra pipeline parameters

Pipeline parameters can be set at the time of the creation of the *PipelineRun*. Each of the pipeline parameters can be mapped and injected into the pipeline jobs. Depending on the type of node and the pipeline runtime environment, the method of injection varies. In our case, **deploy-model-version** is a notebook node, and our runtime is based on **Kubeflow**. In this case, the pipeline parameters are injected as environment variables.

5. Navigate to the **Node Properties** tab to set the properties of the **deploy-model-version** job, as shown in *Figure 5.35*. Notice how we are injecting the **model_version** pipeline parameter:

Figure 5.35 – The node properties of the deploy-model-version node

6. Export the pipeline and import it into your data science project. By now, you should already know how to export the pipeline from the Elyra pipeline editor and import it onto your data science project in OpenShift.

7. Create a *pipeline run* and set the model version to a different version than the one already deployed. This is so that you can verify if the version has been rolled back. *Figure 5.36* shows an example of how the **model_version** pipeline parameter is set during the creation of the *pipeline run*:

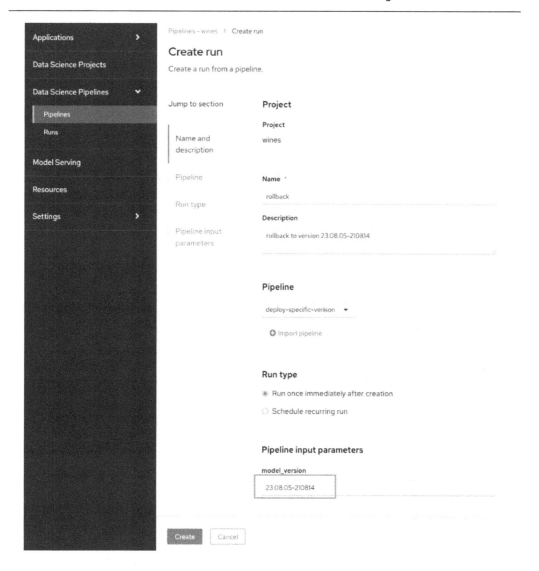

Figure 5.36 – Creating a pipeline run with the pipeline parameter

8. After the pipeline run completes, validate the version number of the model that is deployed in the model server.

9. You have just created a pipeline that can deploy any version of the model on demand. You can use this pipeline to roll back model deployments to any desired version of the model.

At this point, you should be familiar with the Elyra pipeline editor, the model server, and how to deploy the model through the *InferenceService* custom resource. Next, you'll use this knowledge to implement a canary deployment strategy.

Canary model deployment

In the real world, we do not always want to release a new version of the model to the entire population, especially when you have thousands of users using your deployed ML model. **Canary release** or **canary deployment** is a practice of making a staged rollout of services. This is done by releasing the new version of the software alongside the current version while making the new version only available to a limited number of end users. This limits the blast radius in instances where the new version does not perform as expected.

The in-built ingress controller of OpenShift, OpenShift Routes, is based on **HAProxy**, a powerful open source load balancer that can route based on weights. This is also known as **weighted load balancing**. We will use this feature to implement a canary deployment. We will use two model servers running two different versions of our model. Then, we'll configure an OpenShift route that will do the load balancing in front of these two models.

Using the knowledge you gained in the previous sections, create two model servers and manually deploy two different versions of the model onto those servers so that you get the results shown in *Figure 5.37*. When creating these servers, do not tick the **Make deployed models available through an external route** option. You will create an external route manually.

When creating the model servers, use the following names. This is important because you will be creating services that will point to the model-mesh serving pods later:

- `a-wine-server`
- `b-wine-server`

The names of the model servers are also shown in *Figure 5.37*. The name of the model inside the server does not matter in the load balancing context:

Figure 5.37 – Two model servers hosting two versions of the model

Once you have set up the servers and deployed the models, create two services, each pointing to one of the model servers. At this point, we need to create a route that will load balance between these services. To do this, follow these steps:

1. Create a custom *Service* resource that points to the specific pods hosting the specific versions of the models. In the OpenShift console, navigate to **Networking | Services | Create Service**. Replace the contents of the editor with the content of the `service-a.yaml` file under the `/canary-deployment` folder of this book's GitHub repository.

2. Do the same for the `service-b.yaml` file. You should see two services called **wines-a** and **wines-b**, as shown in *Figure 5.38*:

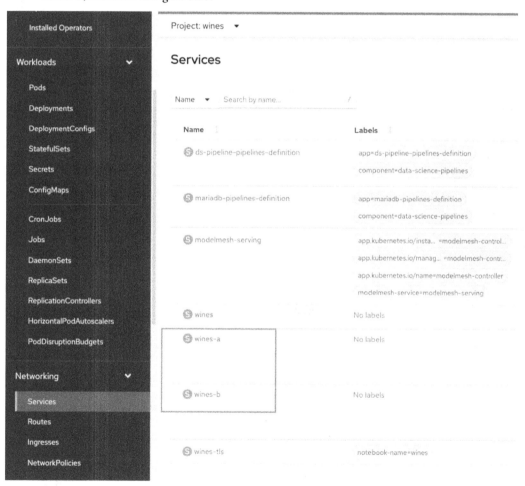

Figure 5.38 – The services under the wines project

3. Now, let's create a *Route* resource that will expose both services in a load-balanced way. In the *Route* definition, we will configure the weights of each service. As an example, we will configure the route to send 77% of the traffic to the *wines-a* service while the remaining 33% is sent to the *wines-b* service. We have prepared a route definition in the `wines-canary-route.yaml` file under the `/canary-deployments` folder of this book's GitHub repository. In the OpenShift console, navigate to **Networking | Routes | Create Route | YAML view**. Then, paste the contents of the `wines-canary-route.yaml` file into the editor. Finally, click **Create**.

4. You have just created a route that load balances between two different versions of your model. Let's get the URL of this route and use it in our `call-model.ipynb` notebook. In the OpenShift console, navigate to **Networking | Routes**. From the list of routes, copy the URL of **wines-canary-route**:

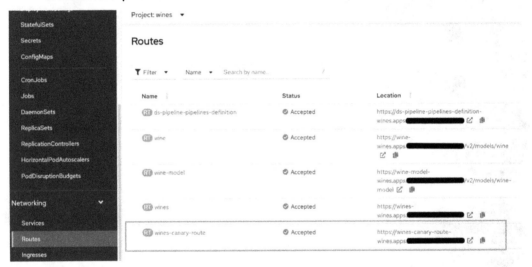

Figure 5.39 – List of routes in the wines project

5. Now, you can use this URL in your `call-model.ipynb` notebook to test your canary setup.

Congratulations! You have just created a **canary deployment** setup for your ML models. This will allow you to slowly roll out the new model to your end users, by adjusting the weights over time, until all of the HTTP traffic goes to the new version of the model. This approach also allows you to implement **A/B testing**.

For the full details of OpenShift routing, refer to the OpenShift documentation at `https://docs.openshift.com/container-platform/4.13/applications/deployments/route-based-deployment-strategies.html`.

Securing model endpoints

When exposing models as APIs, you will want to limit the access to your APIs to certain clients. You will also want to ensure that the APIs are not vulnerable to known **Common Vulnerabilities and Exposures** (**CVE**). When you store your model containers in Red Hat Quay, it will scan the containers to find out any CVE in the libraries and the runtime of your code. Quay is outside the scope of this book but there is plenty of information available on Quay. Packt's *OpenShift Multi-Cluster Management Handbook* contains details about Quay, if you want to know more about it.

The API you deployed earlier in this chapter can be accessed via the HTTPS protocol. This means that OpenShift is already encrypting the traffic using the certificates that have been configured to expose the applications. The configuration of these certificates is outside the scope of this book.

The first step is to restrict access to the API through an authentication mechanism. RHODS uses the OpenShift service account to provide this capability. At the simplest level, think of a service account that associates an identity for your pod, and your model server is running as a pod. A service account exists in each project and provides a flexible way to control API access without sharing a regular user's credentials.

Open the RHODS dashboard and go to the **wines** project. This is the project you created earlier in this chapter. Go to the **Models and model servers** section, where you deployed the model. It will look as follows:

Model Server Name	Serving Runtime	Deployed models	Tokens		
a-wine-server	SeldonMLServer	1	Tokens disabled	Deploy model	⋮
b-wine-server	SeldonMLServer	1	Tokens disabled	Deploy model	⋮
wine	SeldonMLServer	2	Tokens disabled	Deploy model	⋮

Figure 5.40 – List of model servers in the wines project

For the **wine** model server's name, which is the third one in the following screenshot, click on the three dots icon on the rightmost side and select the **Edit model server** option. You will see the following screen. In the **Token authorization** section, tick the **Require token authentication** checkbox to require token authentication for your model server. In the **Service account name** field, enter a service account name for which the token will be generated. In this example, I have entered `wine-auth`. As per the release notes, "users must have "**Admin**" permissions to create a model server with token authorization:"

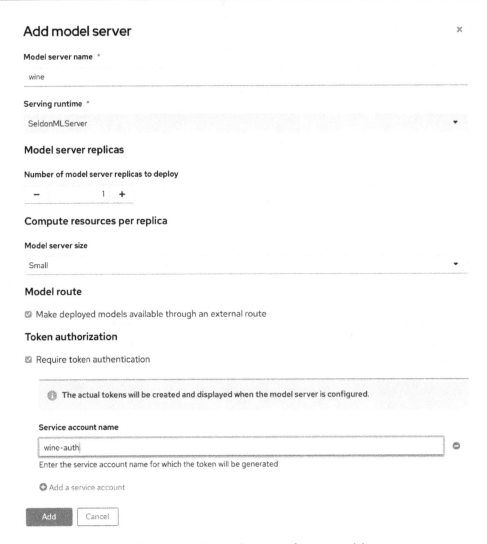

Figure 5.41 – Adding token authorization for your model server

Click **Add**; the generated token will be created. The **Tokens** column of your model server will show the number of tokens associated with your model server, as shown here:

Models and model servers	Add server					
Model Server Name	Serving Runtime	Deployed models		Tokens		
a-wine-server	SeldonMLServer	1		Tokens disabled	Deploy model	⋮
b-wine-server	SeldonMLServer	1		Tokens disabled	Deploy model	⋮
wine	SeldonMLServer	2		1	Deploy model	⋮

Figure 5.42 – The model server list with a token enabled for the wine server

Notice that for the **wine** model server, the screen shows **1** in the **Tokens** column. This specifies the number of service accounts associated with this model server. Note that for other servers, it shows **Tokens disabled**. When you click on the token for the **wine** model server, you'll be taken to the following screen, which shows the token secret. This secret will be used to access the deployed model:

Figure 5.43 – The token secret to copy and use in the inference call

Now, your model can only be accessed with this token. Earlier in this chapter, you accessed your model via the API. Let's see what happens if we try to use our existing code without providing the token. We have created a new notebook for this that's available in this book's GitHub repository. The name of the file is `chapter5/call-model-secure.ipynb`. Note that we are trying to call the model as before and print the response that's received. The output says 403 as the status code. This 403 status code indicates that the server understands the request but refuses to authorize it:

```
# call the wine model without providing the token.
```

```
import requests
import pandas as pd
from urllib3.exceptions import InsecureRequestWarning

data = {'volatile acidity':  [0.17],
        'residual sugar': [1.5],
        'chlorides':  [0.032],
        'total sulfur dioxide': [112.0],
        'sulphates': [0.55],
        'alcohol': [11.4]
        }

wine_0 = pd.DataFrame(data)

inference_request = {
    "inputs": [
        {
            "name": "predict",
            "shape": wine_0.shape,
            "datatype": "FP32",
            "data": wine_0.loc[:].values.tolist()
        }
    ]
}

# Disable SSL Certificate warnings
requests.packages.urllib3.disable_warnings(category=InsecureRequestWarning)

# NOTE: This URL depends on the URL of your OpenShift cluster
endpoint = "https://wine-wines.apps.fmflask2.faisallabs.net/v2/models/wine/infer"
response = requests.post(endpoint, json=inference_request, verify=False)
print(response)
```

```
<Response [403]>
```

Figure 5.44 – A forbidden error occurs if the token has not been passed for inference

Now, run the second part of the same notebook with the token value inserted. Notice that there are two changes; one is the token variable, which holds the token value for me. You must replace this value with the token value for your setup. The second is that we are passing the HTTP header in the POST function call. The two major parts of the code are shown here:

```
token= 'YOUR TOKEN HERE'
response = requests.post(endpoint, json=inference_request,
verify=False, headers={'Authorization': 'Bearer ' + token})
```

When you execute this part of the notebook, you will get a successful response, as shown here:

```
# call the wine model with the token from the Red Hat Data Science Model server token.
```

```
import requests
import pandas as pd

data = {'volatile acidity':  [0.17],
        'residual sugar': [1.5],
        'chlorides':  [0.032],
        'total sulfur dioxide': [112.0],
        'sulphates': [0.55],
        'alcohol': [11.4]
        }

wine_0 = pd.DataFrame(data)

inference_request = {
    "inputs": [
        {
            "name": "predict",
            "shape": wine_0.shape,
            "datatype": "FP32",
            "data": wine_0.loc[:].values.tolist()
        }
    ]
}

endpoint = "https://wine-wines.apps.fmflask2.faisallabs.net/v2/models/wine/infer"
token= 'eyJhbGciOiJSUzI1NiIsImtpZCI6Ino0aUo4RE9ja2UxTy1lQ2lppdjVGelRVR01ScTdkZHd1bk9QOF
response = requests.post(endpoint, json=inference_request, verify=False,
                         headers={'Authorization': 'Bearer ' + token})

print(response)
response.json()
```

```
<Response [200]>
{'model_name': 'wine__isvc-12fe7f5899',
 'outputs': [{'name': 'predict',
   'datatype': 'FP64',
   'shape': [1],
   'data': [6.33739727780333]}]}
```

Figure 5.45 – Successful inference call with the token

With that, your model is ready to serve the universe. OpenShift provides the necessary packaging, scalability, and security capabilities for your model runtime to provide a reliable service for your consumers.

Summary

In this chapter, you experienced the essential tasks surrounding **MLOps**. You built a complete automated pipeline that trains a model, publishes the model to the model store, and deploys it to a model-serving infrastructure, all with RHODS. You also created a pipeline that can perform rollbacks of model deployments. Finally, you implemented a canary deployment setup for your model deployments. These are the essential skills an **MLOps** engineer needs.

One thing to note is that RHODS is evolving fast. New versions are getting released frequently and by the time you are reading this book, the screens may look a bit different and some of the methods of configuring the platform may change a little. We suggest that when performing the exercises in this book, you use *OpenShift version 4.13*.

In the next chapter, we will take you through the operational tasks of **MLOps**. These are the activities that you must perform after deploying a model to production. They include monitoring, logging, and more.

Operating ML Workloads

In the previous chapter, you learned how to automate model deployments through **OpenShift Data Science** (**ODS**) pipelines. This chapter will focus on the operational tasks of **MLOps**. This includes monitoring and logging, using the in-built tools of Red Hat OpenShift Data Science. We will not cover the common OpenShift operation and administration tasks in this chapter as that is beyond the scope of this book. However, we will talk about some of the OpenShift concepts you need to know to understand the topics in this chapter.

The exercises in this chapter require a basic understanding of OpenShift and/or Kubernetes as well as basic knowledge of **Prometheus** time-series databases and **Grafana** visualization dashboards. The following topics will be covered in this chapter:

- Monitoring ML models
- Logging model inference
- Cost optimization

The materials required for this chapter can be found in the GitHub repository of this book. The files that you will need are in the `chapter6` folder.

We will start by talking about **observability**. Some sections can get very technical, so you'd better roll up your sleeves!

Monitoring ML models

Observability is a concept primarily used in the context of systems engineering, computer science, and monitoring complex systems. It refers to the ability to understand and infer the internal state and behavior of a system by examining its external outputs or observables. In simpler terms, it's about gaining insight into how a system operates and performs by observing its outputs or responses.

Monitoring is one of the subjects of observability. It focuses on tracking and measuring predefined metrics and thresholds to ensure that systems and services are running within the expected parameters. It is also referred to as telemetry, akin to how real-time metrics data is collected in mission-critical operations such as launching a rocket to the moon. Unlike **logging**, which focuses on collecting event data for auditing and troubleshooting at a later date, monitoring focuses on real-time events and is focused on metrics information. For example, logging data may contain the actual HTTP request and response payload of an API, while monitoring is focused on the number of requests and the average API latency for a given period in near real time. In addition to typical application monitoring metrics such as latency and throughput, ML models require additional monitoring techniques in order to ensure their performance. This includes model accuracy, model drift, feedback loops, and data quality.

For example, you have deployed a model that predicts the customer churn of a subscription-based service. The model was trained on historical data, and in production, you want to make sure that the model performs as expected. In this case, you want to monitor the quality of data that is being fed to the model at inference time in production and observe the model's confidence level. If most of the time you are getting low-confidence results from the model, then you may need to revisit your training data and re-train the model.

You may also need to monitor the model drift to ensure that the model stays relevant. Say the model typically returns predictions with high confidence, then suddenly, it starts returning low confidence. You want to be informed when this happens because this may be a result of a concept drift.

Prometheus is one of the most popular open source storage options for metrics data. It is a time-series database with its own analytics and query language. Prometheus also comes with a tool that scrapes metrics from a pre-formatted page typically hosted on the same server instance as the application. This is one of the methods that Prometheus uses to collect metrics data. You will learn more about this later.

Grafana is a popular open source data visualization tool that can handle time-series visualizations pretty well. Grafana can read data from various data stores including Prometheus. Grafana is also capable of implementing alerting. This means it can send notifications when certain events occur or when a certain threshold of a metric is hit. You will learn more about this in later sections.

Monitoring implementation can also be tailored to focus on certain areas of the system. In an enterprise IT setting, **system monitoring** usually refers to infrastructure monitoring. This is the near-real-time monitoring of compute resources such as CPU, memory, disk usage, and network anomalies. On the other hand, application monitoring refers to application-specific metrics. This includes request/response latencies, throughput, and error rates. Similarly, monitoring in MLOps is focused on monitoring both the model-serving infrastructure and model performance. Enough talking, let's start implementing observability in our data science project.

Installing and configuring Prometheus and Grafana

To get started with implementing monitoring, we need Prometheus and Grafana. The OpenShift Data Science operator comes with an in-built Prometheus cluster and the model-serving component of ODS is already exposing metrics information by default. This comes pre-installed and pre-configured in your OpenShift cluster when you install the ODS operator. For Grafana, we will install it from **OperatorHub**.

The following steps will guide you through the process of installing and configuring Prometheus and Grafana for your Red Hat OpenShift Data Science cluster:

1. Verify that the Prometheus cluster is installed and is running on your cluster. In your OpenShift web console, navigate to **Workloads | Pods**.

2. Select the **redhat-ods-monitoring** project. You should see that the Prometheus Pods have a **Running** status. If you do not see this, you may need to re-install the Red Hat OpenShift Data Science operator.

3. Navigate to **Networking | Routes**. You should see a route named **rhods-model-monitoring**.

4. Navigate to the route URL. This is the external URL of your Prometheus instance and will take you to the Prometheus landing page.

5. In the top menu, select **Status | Service Discovery**. You will see the list of `ServiceMonitor` used by this instance of Prometheus, as shown in *Figure 6.1*. `ServiceMonitor` are Kubernetes custom resources used by Prometheus to determine which *services* it needs to scrape metrics data from.

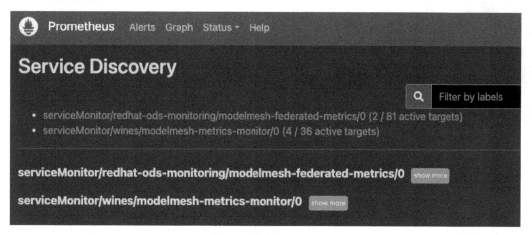

Figure 6.1 – Prometheus Service Discovery page

6. Now that you have verified the Prometheus installation in your cluster, let's install Grafana. In your OpenShift web console, navigate to **OperatorHub**. Search for Grafana and install the Grafana operator. You already know how to install operators from OperatorHub. Install the Grafana operator in its own namespace called **grafana**. Create the project if it does not exist. Refer to *Figure 6.2*.

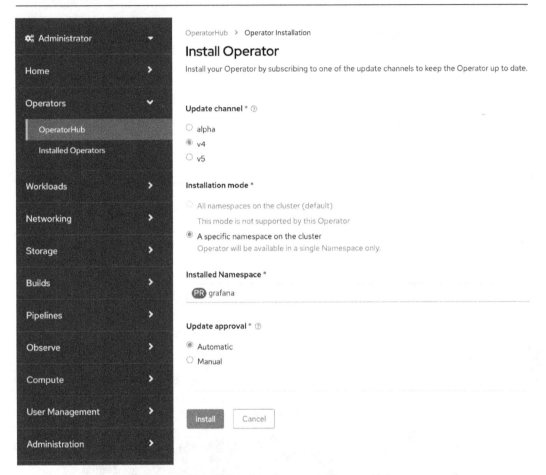

Figure 6.2 – Grafana install screen in OperatorHub

7. Click **Install** and wait for the operator installation to complete.

8. Once the operator is installed, create a new Grafana instance by applying the `grafana.yaml` file to your OpenShift cluster. You can use the plus (+) button at the top-right corner of the OpenShift web console. You can find this file in the `chapter6/monitoring` folder. This will create a new instance of the Grafana server on your OpenShift cluster.

9. `grafana-datasource.yaml` will create a new Grafana data source configuration pointing to the ODS Prometheus instance. However, in order for Grafana to authenticate to the Prometheus database, we need to give it an access token. Retrieve the token from a Kubernetes **Secret** called **rhods-prometheus-operator-token-xxxxx** under the **redhat-ods-monitoring** project. This is the token of the **rhods-prometheus-operator** service account. We will use this token because this service account has access to the Prometheus database. In a production setup, you may want to create a dedicated service account for accessing Prometheus. Take a look at *Figure 6.3* to see where to find this Secret.

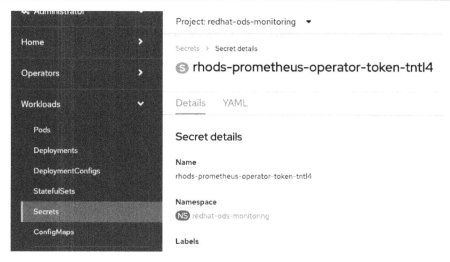

Figure 6.3 – Prometheus service account Secret

10. Copy the value of the **Token** field of the Secret and paste it in `grafana-datasource.yaml` replacing the `<<TOKEN>>` placeholder in the file. Your YAML file should look like the screenshot in *Figure 6.4*.

```
1  apiVersion: integreatly.org/v1alpha1
2  kind: GrafanaDataSource
3  metadata:
4    name: ods-monitoring-prometheus
5    namespace: grafana
6  spec:
7    datasources:
8      - access: proxy
9        editable: true
10       isDefault: true
11       jsonData:
12         httpHeaderName1: Authorization
13         timeInterval: 5s
14         tlsSkipVerify: true
15       name: ods-monitoring-prometheus
16       secureJsonData:
17         httpHeaderValue1: >-
18           Bearer
eyJhbGciOiJSUzI1NiIsImtpZCI6Ino0aUo4RE9ja2UxTy1lQ2lpdjVGelRVR01ScTdkZHd1bk9QOF9LRURtSEUifQ
aWNlYWNjb3VudC9uYW1lc3BhY2UiOiJyZWRoYXQtb2RzLW1vbml0b3JpbmciLCJrdWJlcm5ldGVzLlNlcnZpY2
0bnRsNCIsImt1YmVybmV0ZXMuaW8vc2VydmljZWFjY291bnQvc2VydmljZS1hY2NvdW50Lm5hbWUiOiJyaG9kcy1wc
NlLWFjY291bnQudWlkIjoiY2UzNTEzMDItM2Q1Yy00ZTQ5LWIzNTUtY2FiZWZhNWRkMWU3Iiwic3ViIjoic3lzdGVt
W9wZXJhdGd9yIn0.oMgOZgCC2r-yxdeDYbFvd_NKZ2lHv-4JfHZgAtLCCLYm1iXN-Tvv8UpxhBwERosnV3NqxhFPWPi
Ab6luQPD2uQdARhyt9lgGwvx8d8w48xoCHpxELApRNpKkmNYR7PphRHNV17IN9GoGbpBkx4nEXXowAEKE1QXqvmgxc
v240mp145UmW87hn6y_DPvTWTCEnH5vPNVolDtRbSvMHZf4wcPgsc9bd77GPOdymMGDK_AFscShx8amLLldeBCu_aP
lUj-0ai9N2W-1jUmfytMKkQUHZhcGWoMxUbz2UhYDCGRjeuacghIrztwtqWjoG5-O-Nh73aZz9i7kqTqBHzwhrsDR0
haalwEQHojBfBeZTQmbNtho7jXrF8OxQSHpc2leyYuKSThmwn3iiP88SaTYGZfw6Q3l4LZmE6pstilWvAW5i5AO6RR
8Gg4GSWbRDDO0ebLO65MoMrt7mZS9Ugy4mZCbj8Q
19         type: prometheus
20         url: 'https://rhods-model-monitoring.redhat-ods-monitoring.svc.cluster.local'
21     name: ods-monitoring-prometheus.yaml
```

Figure 6.4 – grafana-datasource.yaml file with token

11. Then apply the `grafana-dashboard.yaml` file to your OpenShift cluster. This will create a predefined dashboard on your Grafana server. We have prepared this Grafana dashboard for the purpose of showing an example of how you can create charts out of the Prometheus data produced by ODS monitoring. Feel free to edit the dashboard and experiment with it. You need to understand the basic concepts of the Grafana dashboard and the Prometheus query language to edit the charts in the example dashboard. We will not cover these topics in the book as they are beyond the book's scope. The next thing you need to do is to expose the Grafana dashboard so that it can be accessed outside the cluster.

12. Create a route to expose the Grafana service and make it accessible outside the cluster. Navigate to **Networking** | **Routes** | **Create Route**. Refer to *Figure 6.5* for the route configuration.

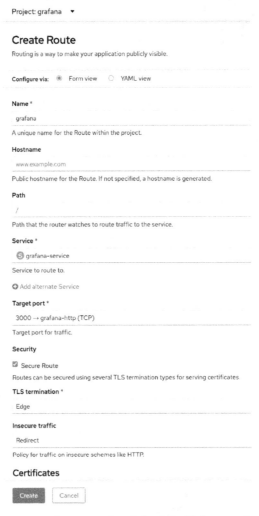

Figure 6.5 – Route creation dialog for a Grafana service

13. Navigate to the route URL. You should see the Grafana login page.

14. To log in, you need to use the Grafana credentials stored in a Secret called **grafana-admin-credentials** under the **grafana** project.

15. On the Grafana home page, from the top menu, navigate to **General | grafana | Modelmesh Monitoring Dashboard**. If everything is working, you should see a Grafana dashboard displayed, as shown in *Figure 6.6*.

Congratulations! You have just created a Grafana dashboard for your model-serving infrastructure. This will give you near-real-time insights into the model-serving infrastructure and your model performance.

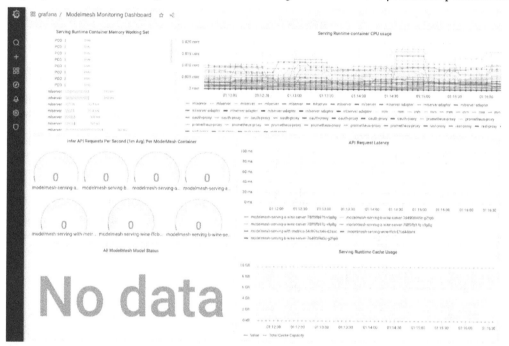

Figure 6.6 – Modelmesh Monitoring Dashboard

To test whether the dashboard is working, use the same call-model notebook you used in *Chapter 5* to invoke the model inference call several times and observe how the dashboard moves as the number of model inference calls increases.

The model-serving infrastructure of Red Hat OpenShift Data Science is based on **ModelMesh**, a general-purpose model-serving runtime. It uses **ModelMesh-Serving** as the controller for managing ModelMesh. ModelMesh and ModelMesh-Serving together work very similarly to the ServiceMesh architecture, treating your ML models like microservices. Both the ModelMesh and ModelMesh-Serving projects are open source and are well documented. See the ModelMesh references at the end of this chapter.

Logging inference calls

Logging is an essential part of any software architecture. We use logs to recall and investigate what happened to the system in the past. Unlike monitoring, logs are more focused on the events that occurred in the system in the past with the objective of providing the capability to look back on or perform an audit of past events.

Logging in MLOps is no different. However, there are a few aspects of logging that are more common in ML model inference than in traditional software. Here are some of the properties that we need to look out for in ML model inference logging:

- **Unstructured data**: In some cases, the data you input into the inference call may not always be simple JSON-formatted text; it could be an image, video, or audio as well. This kind of unstructured data may require a different kind of storage system for logs.

- **Non-deterministic behavior**: Some models, depending on the algorithm used, may not always return the same output for the same given input in the past. **Stochastic** models, for example, learn from historical data and improve over time. It may be necessary to log or record these changes in input and output pairs over time.

- **Bias and fairness logging**: In ML applications, it's important to log metrics related to bias, fairness, and ethics to ensure that models are not making discriminatory or biased decisions.

It is also important to note that logging in MLOps depends on the capability of the model-serving runtime. In OpenShift Data Science, the serving runtime is based on ModelMesh. It has a class of objects called **payload processors** that can be configured in the container's environment variable. However, as of the time of writing, there is currently no way to explicitly configure the model-serving logging within the OpenShift Data Science web user interface. **RHODS** is still evolving, and there is no doubt that this feature will be added in the near future.

One of the available payload processors in ModelMesh is called a **logging payload processor**. This will log the inference requests and responses to the default log appender, which is, in the container's case, the standard output stream. In other words, by enabling this processor, you are logging the request and response for inferences to the standard output stream.

To enable this payload processor, we need to edit the `Deployment` manifest of the model server called `wine` and set the variable as the following:

```
MM_PAYLOAD_PROCESSORS=logger://*
```

The `logger://*` value includes all the model inference endpoints of the model server. You may also choose to log only certain model endpoints in cases where you deployed multiple models on the same model server. The variable also accepts a whitespace-separated list of payload processors.

Another type of payload processor available in ModelMesh is called `RemotePayloadProcessor`. This payload processor performs an HTTP post request to a given URL every time an inference request occurs. This allows you to post request and response payloads to applications such as **Elasticsearch**.

To enable this payload processor along with the existing one, set the value of the variable as the following:

```
MM_PAYLOAD_PROCESSORS=logger://* http://some-url-that-accepts-post
```

An example of this variable being set is shown in *Figure 6.7*.

Figure 6.7 – Payload processor environment variable

While the model-serving component can write inference payload logs to the standard output stream and to an HTTP endpoint, it is also important that you enable OpenShift's login stack to aggregate all the container logs in a central repository, including the logs of the model-serving containers. You can do this by installing either of these operators from OperatorHub:

- **Red Hat OpenShift Logging**: This is the older logging stack of OpenShift based on Elasticsearch, **FluentD**, and **Kibana**.

- **Loki Operator**: This is a newer technology stack that was introduced in OpenShift 4.10. This is based on **Loki**.

By enabling either of these OpenShift logging subsystems, you will have the ability to query the logs of all Pods in OpenShift centrally. We will not show you how to install this operator as you already know how to install operators. To further understand the logging subsystem of OpenShift, you may refer to the OpenShift Logging documentation.

Voilà! You now have a better understanding of logging in the context of MLOps and OpenShift. Now, let's take a look at other things you need to look out for when running ML workloads.

Optimizing cost

When it comes to managing an OpenShift cluster, it's not just about making sure your applications run smoothly; it's also about keeping a close eye on your cloud infrastructure costs. OpenShift is incredibly powerful, but if you're not careful, it can lead to unnecessary overspending. In this guide, we'll dive into some practical strategies to help you fine-tune your OpenShift cluster, so you can strike that perfect balance between having the resources you need and keeping your budget under control. From optimizing how you allocate resources to scaling your cluster intelligently, these practices will empower you to make the most of your Kubernetes setup without breaking the bank:

- **Rightsize resources**: Take a closer look at the resource requirements of your applications running in Pods. Adjust the allocated CPU and memory to match the actual needs of each application. Avoid overallocating resources, which can lead to unnecessary costs. Although there are predefined sizes in Red Hat OpenShift Data Science, these sizes can also be customized. You can even create your own sizes. This can be done by editing a custom resource called **OdhDashboardConfig**. This is where both the notebook sizes and model server sizes are configured. *Figure 6.8* shows where to find this custom resource.

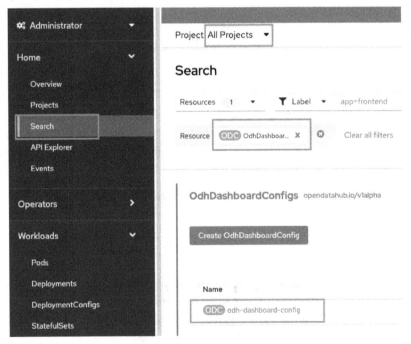

Figure 6.8 – Searching for a custom resource called OdhDashboardConfig

Depending on the needs of your data science or ML project, you may want to change the default sizes of the workbenches and model servers and create your own custom sizes. This can be done by changing the **OdhDashboardConfig** resource. By default, this resource contains the following configuration for notebook and model server sizes:

```
modelServerSizes:
  - name: Small
    resources:
      limits:
        cpu: '2'
        memory: 8Gi
      requests:
        cpu: '1'
        memory: 4Gi
  - name: Medium
    resources:
      limits:
        cpu: '8'
        memory: 10Gi
      requests:
        cpu: '4'
        memory: 8Gi
  - name: Large
    resources:
      limits:
        cpu: '10'
        memory: 20Gi
      requests:
        cpu: '6'
        memory: 16Gi
notebookSizes:
  - name: Small
    resources:
      limits:
        cpu: '2'
        memory: 8Gi
      requests:
        cpu: '1'
        memory: 8Gi
  - name: Medium
    resources:
      limits:
        cpu: '6'
        memory: 24Gi
```

```
      requests:
        cpu: '3'
        memory: 24Gi
- name: Large
  resources:
    limits:
      cpu: '14'
      memory: 56Gi
    requests:
      cpu: '7'
      memory: 56Gi
- name: X Large
  resources:
    limits:
      cpu: '30'
      memory: 120Gi
    requests:
      cpu: '15'
      memory: 120Gi
```

Changing this configuration will not change the existing notebooks and model servers. This will only change the available sizing options when creating workbenches and model servers from the ODS user interface.

- **Autoscale nodes**: Set up automatic scaling for your cluster nodes. This means that the cluster will intelligently add or remove nodes based on the workload. During periods of high traffic, it scales up to handle the load, and during quieter times, it scales down to save on resources and costs. The **cluster autoscaling** feature of OpenShift is very well documented. Refer to the cluster autoscaling documentation of OpenShift for more information.

- **Autoscale Pods**: Optimize the way you schedule and distribute Pods across nodes. The goal is to maximize the number of Pods running on each node without causing resource conflicts. OpenShift provides features such as **horizontal pod autoscaling** (**HPA**) to help you achieve this efficiently. We also showed you an example of the HPA resource in the previous chapter.

- **Storage and network optimization**: Select the right storage options for your data based on its importance and usage. Choose high-performance storage for critical data and more cost-effective options for less critical data.

Minimize data transfer between Pods and services by keeping them in close proximity. This reduces data transfer costs and helps your cluster operate more efficiently. One way to do this is to run your data storage applications, such as databases and object storage, inside OpenShift or at least within the same cloud account.

- **Use Reserved and Spot Instances**: Consider purchasing reserved instances for your nodes if you're using a cloud environment. They offer cost savings compared to on-demand instances, particularly for predictable workloads.

    When possible, take advantage of spot instances, which are usually more cost-effective for non-critical workloads, even though they can be preempted.

> **Note**
>
> Refer to the AWS EC2 instances comparison at `https://docs.aws.amazon.com/AWSEC2/latest/UserGuide/instance-purchasing-options.html`.

- **Set resource quotas**: Define resource quotas to prevent runaway resource usage within your cluster. These quotas ensure that individual applications don't consume more than their fair share of resources. Resource quotas can also be set at a project level. You may want to limit the resources allocated to certain data science projects.

    You can set these limits in the OpenShift web console under **Administration | Limit Ranges**.

- **Monitor and adjust**: Use tools and services that help you keep an eye on your OpenShift cluster's costs. Regularly review reports and usage patterns to identify areas where cost savings can be realized.

    Set budget thresholds and alerts to receive timely notifications when your costs exceed predefined limits, as this allows you to take corrective actions as needed.

    One tool that can help you achieve this in OpenShift is the **Cost Management Metrics Operator**. You can install this operator on your cluster. This will then calculate the estimated costs based on the monitoring metrics data of OpenShift. The cost reports are published through Red Hat Hybrid Cloud Console (`https://console.redhat.com`) under your Red Hat account.

- **Optimizing pipelines**: Simplify your MLOps pipelines and ensure that they efficiently build and deploy containers. Remove or clean up pipelines that are no longer used. Streamlining these processes can help minimize the costs associated with builds and storage.

- **Continuously review and adjust**: Remember that cost optimization is an ongoing effort. Regularly assess your cluster's resource utilization and costs, adapting your strategies as your workloads evolve and your requirements change. Collaboration between your technical and financial teams is key to long-term cost optimization.

    The monitoring component that you have installed and configured in this chapter can also provide inputs to the continuous review of cost. For example, if you find that a model server with eight CPUs allocated is only getting two inference calls per second, then you may want to adjust the size of the model server.

By following these practices and keeping a vigilant eye on your cluster's performance and costs, you can ensure that your Kubernetes setup is both effective and budget-friendly for your organization.

Summary

This chapter focused on the operational tasks related to running and serving ML models on OpenShift and OpenShift Data Science. You have learned that Red Hat OpenShift Data Science comes with a Prometheus instance. You have also learned how to set up Grafana to visualize the Prometheus data.

We have talked about the importance of logging and how it is different from monitoring and traditional software application logging. You have also learned how to enable the ModelMesh payload processors to achieve payload logging.

We have also learned that the current version of ODS does not yet contain a feature for configuring the logging dimension of model servers through the web console.

As part of your learning, we encourage you to experiment with the configurations beyond what was described in the book. There is a lot more to learn about Grafana and Prometheus. You can explore other metrics in Prometheus and create custom dashboards in Grafana. We also encourage you to experiment with logging and drift detection techniques beyond what you saw in this chapter.

Finally, we have given you some tips on optimizing the cost of running OpenShift and helped visualize the cost.

In the next chapter, we'll recall all the things that you have learned by creating an example ML project from scratch using Red Hat OpenShift Data Science.

References

Model serving via model mesh: `https://kserve.github.io/website/0.8/modelserving/mms/modelmesh/overview/`

Alibi library to explain the model outcome: `https://kserve.github.io/website/0.8/modelserving/detect/alibi_detect/alibi_detect/`

How OpenShift scales the cluster: `https://docs.openshift.com/container-platform/4.13/machine_management/applying-autoscaling.html`

Building a Face Detector Using the Red Hat ML Platform

In the previous chapter of this book, you learned how the Red Hat platform enables you to build and deploy ML models. In this chapter, you will see that model is just one part of the puzzle. You have to collect data and process it before it can be fed to the model and you can get a useful response. You will see how the Red Hat platform enables you to build and deploy all the components required for a real-world application.

The aim of this chapter is to introduce you to how other Red Hat services on the same OpenShift platform provide a complete ecosystem for your needs. In this chapter, you will learn about the following:

- Building and deploying a TensorFlow model to detect faces
- Capturing a video feed from your local laptop
- Storing the results in Redis, running on the OpenShift platform
- Generating an alert when the model detects a face in the feed
- Cost optimization strategies for the OpenShift platform

Architecting a human face detector system

We will start by defining the business use case, its utility, and an architectural diagram of how the components work together.

The idea is to collect a video feed from where you can detect multiple objects and respond accordingly. For example, in our case, we are detecting a human face in a real-time video feed. This system could capture the feed from the front of your house and work as a security system. Or, you can apply the same workflow to detect potholes on the road through a continuous video feed collected by a car.

Once the camera captures the feed, it sends the video frame by frame to an application running on your OpenShift cluster, which then calls the model for inference. Once the model detects a face, the calling application displays and stores the results in a Redis cache (you can further enhance the application to store the results in a database), from where you can display the result or generate an alert. The backend application and the alert generation app would also be hosted on the same Red Hat platform, but the exercise here will not cover the alerting application.

By doing the exercises in the chapter, you will see how different components work together as a system and how the Red Hat OpenShift platform can scale each of the components of the system from end to end, from model training to inferencing.

The architecture diagram in *Figure 7.1* shows the different components of the inferencing system.

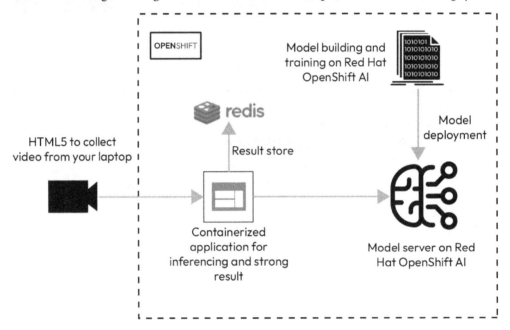

Figure 7.1 – The face detector architecture

In the remainder of this chapter, we will build this architecture. We will start with training our model, and then configure and install Redis. We will then build and deploy the containerized application that will make the inference call and print the results. Lastly, we will build an HTML page that captures the video from your laptop and sends the data to the application running on the same OpenShift platform. Let us start with training the model.

Training a model for face detection

In this section, you will use a pre-trained model to build your own model for detecting a human face in a picture. This may be a simple example but we have chosen it for a reason. Our aim is to show you how different components work together in such a system while being able to test it from any laptop with a webcam. You can enhance and rebuild the model for more complicated use cases if needed.

You will use Google's EfficientNet, a highly efficient convolutional neural network, as the base pre-trained model. With pre-trained models, you do not need a huge amount of data to train the model for your use case. This will save you both time and compute resources. This method of reusing pre-trained models is also called **transfer learning**.

Because this model is specifically designed for image classification, in this example, we will be using it to classify whether an image contains a human face, a human finger, or something else. As a result, we will achieve the objective of detecting a human face in the image.

To start with, let's create a new data science project in Red Hat OpenShift Data Science. You already know how to do this from previous chapters. Let's name the new project `face-detection`. Once you have created the new project, create a workbench and call it `face-detection`. Use the workbench configuration detailed in *Figure 7.2*.

Property	Value
Name	`face-detection`
Notebook Image selection	TensorFlow
Version selection	2023.1 (Recommended) or latest
Deployment size	Medium
Cluster storage/name	`face-detection`
Persistent storage size	20 GiB
Use data connection	Yes
Data connections / Name	`minio-face-detection`
Data connections / Access key	`Minio`
Data connections / Secret key	`minio123`
Data connections / Endpoint	`http://minio-ml-workshop.minio.svc.cluster.local:9000`
Data connections / Region	(Leave empty)
Data connections / Bucket	`face-detection`

Figure 7.2 – Workbench configuration

Your new workbench should start in a few seconds and your data science project should look as in the screenshot in *Figure 7.3*, showing the workbench, storage, and data connections.

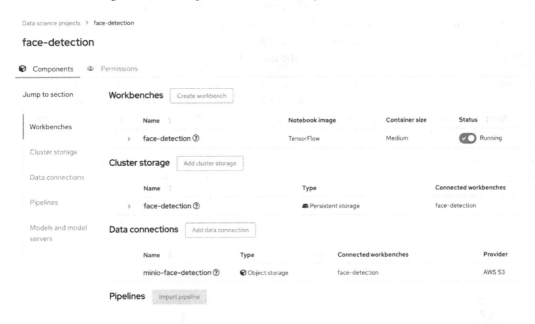

Figure 7.3 – Data science project configuration

Now, open the workbench and start the model training workflow. Clone this book's GitHub repository. In the `chapter7` folder, open the notebook file named `face-detector-training.ipynb` under the `training` subfolder.

In the same directory where the notebook is located, there are two ZIP files, `data.zip` and `test.zip`, which contain the training data and test data, respectively. Go through the cells of the notebook to understand the steps. Run each cell to manually execute the training process and manually evaluate whether the test results are acceptable. If everything works, the validation accuracy should be between 80% and 90%, while the testing process should return all correct predictions.

Once you are satisfied with the results, you can then proceed with adding this training to a pipeline. But before you do that, place the dataset in the right location. Putting this file in the same directory as the notebook is expected when running the training manually from within the notebook workbench. However, the `data.zip` and `test.zip` files will not be available on the pipeline server. Therefore, we need to host these files on our **S3** storage. The following steps will guide you through what is required to automate the training workflow with pipelines:

1. In MinIO, create a directory called `dataset` under the `face-detection` bucket.

2. Upload the data.zip and test.zip files to the /dataset path of the face-detection bucket. You may also want to version this dataset as you wish using **Pachyderm** to test the knowledge you gained in the previous chapter.

3. Modify the face-detector-training.ipynb notebook so that it downloads the data.zip and test.zip files from the S3 bucket.

4. Then, add a step in the notebook that will upload or publish the model to the project's S3 bucket. We assume that you already know the process of doing this as you learned this in *Chapter 6*. This involves creating a bucket to hold your model versions. You can use the same bucket name you used when creating the workbench data connection, face-detection.

Take note that the model you have created this time is a **TensorFlow** model, which usually ends with an .h5 filename extension.

If everything works, you should have a pipeline that looks as in the screenshot in *Figure 7.4*.

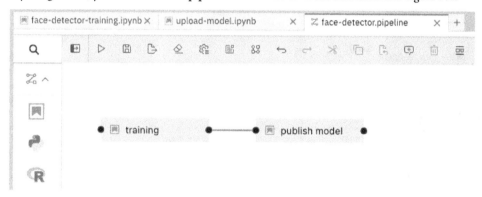

Figure 7.4 – Pipeline with training and publish model tasks

Before we can export and run this pipeline, you need to configure the data science project first. You need to create a pipeline server that you will use to execute pipelines. We covered the detailed steps of creating a pipeline server in *Chapter 5*. Go ahead and create a PipelineServer in the face-detection data science project.

Configure your notebook runtime to add the data science pipeline server you have just created. We also covered the detailed steps of configuring runtimes in *Chapter 5*. If you do everything correctly, you should be able to export the pipeline, import it to your data science project pipelines on ODS, and run it successfully, as shown in *Figure 7.5*.

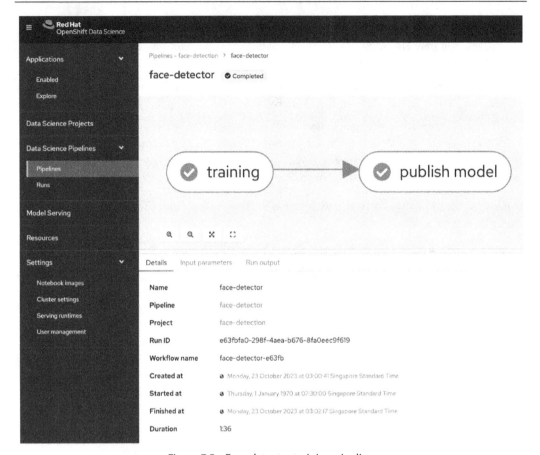

Figure 7.5 – Face detector training pipeline

You should now have a new version of the face detector model uploaded to the S3 bucket of your data science project. Before you can extend this pipeline to include a deployment, we first need to create a model server. The next section will take you through the creation of an **Open Visual Inference and Neural network Optimization (OpenVINO)** model server.

Deploying the model

In the previous section, you built the TensorFlow model to detect a face and create a pipeline to automate the model training and model publishing. In this section, you will see how to deploy the model using the OpenVINO format.

OpenVINO is an open source toolkit developed by Intel. It is designed to accelerate the deployment of deep learning models on Intel hardware, including CPUs, GPUs, Field-**Programmable Gate Arrays (FPGAs)**, and **Vision Processing Units (VPUs)**.

The primary goal of OpenVINO is to provide a unified and efficient platform for deploying computer vision and deep learning applications across a range of Intel processors. It optimizes and accelerates inference workloads, making it suitable for a variety of applications, such as image and video analysis, facial recognition, and object detection. The OpenVINO model format is an intermediate format. Think of byte code in Java, which helps to run an optimal inferencing process on the available hardware. The OpenVINO model consists of an `.xml` file, containing information about the model's architecture, and a `.bin` file, containing the weights and biases of the model.

In the previous chapters, you deployed the model using Seldon Core. However, in this chapter, you will deploy the model trained in the previous section using OpenVINO. This is to show different options of hosting your model for inferencing and the flexibility of the Red Hat OpenShift Data Science platform.

Let's start with defining a new model server by clicking on the **Add Model Server** option in your new Red Hat OpenShift Data Science project, `face-detection`. Put the model server name as `face-detection` and the serving runtime as **OpenVINO Model Server**, as shown.

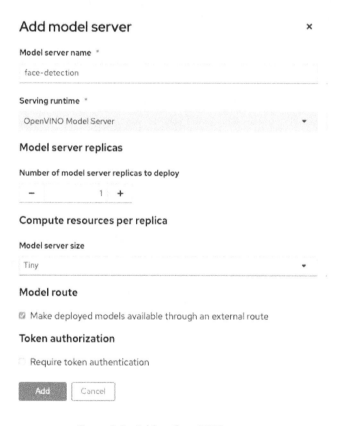

Figure 7.6 – Add an OpenVINO server

Now that you have an OpenVINO model server running, the next step is to convert the TensorFlow model file into the OpenVINO model file format. Open the chapter07/convert-model-openvino.py file from the GitHub repo of this book in your workbench. Assuming that the TensorFlow model file was created in the previous section and is available on your MinIO S3 server, there are three major parts of the conversion code:

1. First, you need to install the OpenVINO module, import the libraries, and initialize the OpenVINO (ov) component:

    ```
    !pip install openvino
    import openvino as ov
    import tensorflow as tf
    core = ov.Core()
    ```

2. The second is to convert the TensorFlow model file into **Protocol Buffers (Protobuf)** format. This step is optional as you may have already saved the model in the Protobuf format during model training. This will save the model binaries into the model folder:

    ```
    import tensorflow as tf
    model = tf.keras.models.load_model('model.h5') tf.saved_model.
    save(model,'model')
    ```

3. The last part is to save the model in OpenVINO format. This will generate two files, one called model.xml, which contains the model architecture, and another file called model.bin, which contains the weights and biases:

    ```
    # reading from the model file that was saved during the training
    notebook
    ov_model = ov.convert_model("./model")
    ov.save_model(ov_model, 'openvino/model.xml')
    ```

If everything works, you should now have a folder called openvino, with two files in it, in your workspace.

Now that you know how to convert a TensorFlow model file into an OpenVINO model, edit your training notebook and your pipeline so that the model that you upload to an S3 bucket in your training pipeline will be in OpenVINO format. If your training pipeline is successful, you should see the two files uploaded to your S3 bucket, as shown in *Figure 7.7*.

Figure 7.7 – OpenVINO model files in MinIO

If your pipeline failed because it cannot find the binary files, check whether the training node in your pipeline is configured with a declaration of the output file, as shown in *Figure 7.8*.

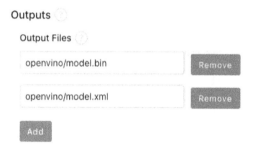

Figure 7.8 – Output files declaration in the pipeline training node

Now that you have the model available in an S3 bucket, let's validate the uploaded model and test your model server. To do this, deploy the model to the model server named `face-detection`. Open the Red Hat OpenShift Data Science portal, go to the `face-detection` model server, and select the **Deploy Model** option. Fill in the values and point the path to the S3 folder containing the `model.bin` and `model.xml` files, as shown in *Figure 7.9*.

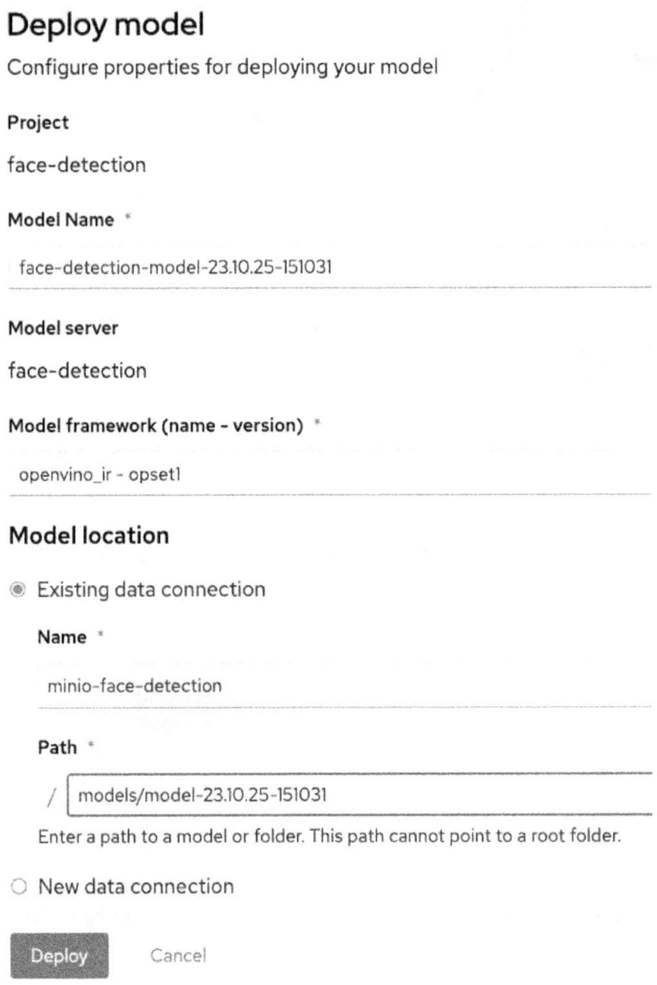

Deploy model

Configure properties for deploying your model

Project

face-detection

Model Name *

face-detection-model-23.10.25-151031

Model server

face-detection

Model framework (name - version) *

openvino_ir - opset1

Model location

◉ Existing data connection

Name *

minio-face-detection

Path *

/ | models/model-23.10.25-151031

Enter a path to a model or folder. This path cannot point to a root folder.

○ New data connection

Deploy   Cancel

Figure 7.9 – Deploy model dialog using the OpenVINO model server

Give a model a name, such as `face-detection-ser-ov`, and make sure you select the right model server name, which is `face-detection`. Select the `openvio_ir - opset1` framework, where `ir` stands for intermediate representation. Hit **Deploy** and your model will be deployed on the model server. You can verify whether the model was deployed successfully by checking whether there is a green check mark under **Status**.

Figure 7.10 – Model deployment status

This means that your model is now deployed and is ready for inference calls.

Using the knowledge you gained about automating model deployment in *Chapter 6*, enhance the pipeline so that it contains a step or node that will deploy the model automatically. We have prepared the files that you will need for the deployment automation, and they are available under the `/chapter7/deploy` folder.

Validating the deployed model

In the previous chapters, you used HTTP to make calls to deployed models. In this section, you will see how you can make the call using the **gRPC Remote Procedure Call (gRPC)** protocol.

gRPC is an open source remote procedure call framework developed by Google. It is designed for building efficient and high-performance **Application Programming Interfaces (APIs)** with support for multiple programming languages. gRPC uses the HTTP/2 protocol for communication and Protobuf as the interface definition language. gRPC is more efficient when it comes to bidirectional streaming between the client and server than standard RESTful APIs. This is why it is more popular for machine vision applications.

In this example, you don't want the model to be exposed to the world. You will write a new Python application (in the later sections) that will receive data from the camera and perform the inferencing. The Python application will be exposed to the internet, and it will also be hosted on the same OpenShift platform, which provides the basis for running all the components of your application.

Let's see what the calling code will look like. Open the chapter7/validate-deployed-model.py file and you will see the following code. I will show part of the code here; you can find the full code at the GitHub link mentioned previously.

The code uses the Triton client library to make the call. The first part is where the imports have been made. Notice the modelmesh-serving.wines.svc.cluster.local:8033 value passed to the triton_client variable. This is the OpenShift service that is exposed by the model server for the gRPC endpoint.

The second part is defining the input and output arrays. Notice that we are using the NumPy random number generation functionality to create a random array with a 256,256,3 shape. This is the expected shape of the input array, which is a 256,256 image with three channels for RGB. So, every image is identified by this array.

The last part is where you make the call, which results in an array of numbers containing the confidence level for each category on which you have trained your model. So, if you have trained the model for identifying a face and not a face, this means the returned array will have two numbers capturing the confidence level for each category. If you have multiple categories, the array size will be greater. For example, if I trained my model for three categories, such as face, hand, and background, then the output array will have three values, as shown in the following code block. You can see the first one has a confidence of >99% and the model suggests that this frame belongs to the first category:

```
[[0.99384874 0.00328289 0.00286839]]
```

Here is the code:

```
import tritonclient.grpc as grpcclient
import numpy as np

try:
keepalive_options = grpcclient.KeepAliveOptions(...)
triton_client = grpcclient.InferenceServerClient(
url='modelmesh-serving.wines.svc.cluster.local:8033',..)

model_name = "face-detection-ser-ov"
inputs = []
outputs = []
inputs.append(grpcclient.InferInput('input_1', [1, 256, \
    256, 3], "FP32"))
```

```
input0_data = np.random.randn(1, 256, 256, 3).astype(np.float32)


# Initialize the data
inputs[0].set_data_from_numpy(input0_data)

outputs.append(grpcclient.InferRequestedOutput('pred'))

# Test with outputs
results = triton_client.infer(model_name=model_name,
inputs=inputs,
outputs=outputs)
print(results)
# Get the output arrays from the results
output0_data = results.as_numpy('pred')
print(output0_data)
```

Congratulations! You have deployed the model and can call the model via gRPC. Before we move on to deploying an app that takes camera data and makes inference calls – hosted on the OpenShift platform, of course – we will first deploy Redis on the OpenShift cluster to store a counter of the number of faces detected.

Installing Redis on Red Hat OpenShift

Redis is a super-fast in-memory database. Redis provides a key-value store with different data structures, such as lists, for the applications to use. In our case, the video generates a lot of frames and our application will infer these frames and keep a count of frames/images with faces. So, we decided to use Redis to keep an atomic counter.

OpenShift will host the Redis server. You will find the complete non-production Redis setup in the `chapter7/redis/redis-server.yaml` file. Open the file and paste it into the OpenShift GUI while you are in the `face-detection` project. Hit the **Create** button and you will have a running Redis cluster on your platform. The following screenshot shows `redis-server.yaml` in the OpenShift UI.

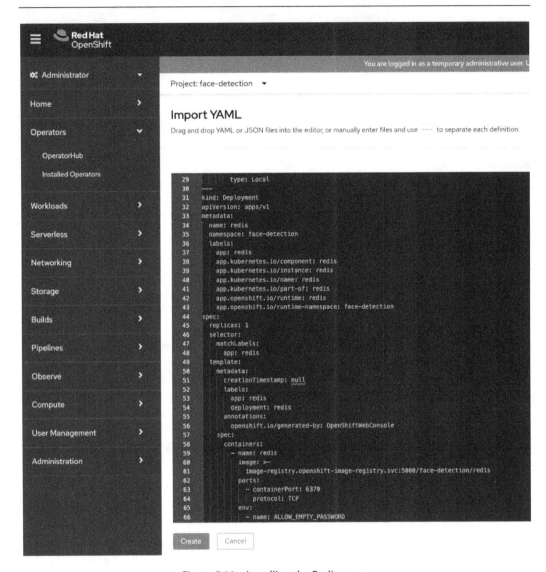

Figure 7.11 – Installing the Redis server

Validate that the server is running by checking the **services** section of the OpenShift console within the `wines` project, identify the Pods, and validate from the logs that the server is running. You will see an output like in the following screenshot.

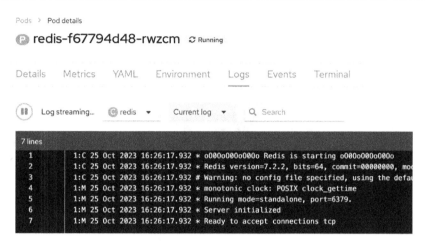

Figure 7.12 – Validating that the Redis server is running

Now that we have deployed Redis, the next step is to deploy the inferencing application.

Building and deploying the inferencing application

Before we dive deep into the inferencing application, let's understand the application components. Our aim is to collect information from a camera, such as the video camera on your laptop, and then send it to the application, where the application will make a call to your model and see whether a face has been detected.

The video-capturing application (we call it the frontend) will capture the video and send every tenth frame as an array of 256-by-256 image to the server via HTTP. The server (or the backend application) will receive the frame or image and make an inference call to the model. The backend service will also keep a Redis-based counter, and when a face is detected, the application will increment the face counter in the Redis database. The backend service will also expose another HTTP service to read the value of the counter, which will then be displayed in the frontend service. Conceptually, it looks as in the following figure.

Do note that all these components, the model and the Redis database, are on the same OpenShift platform.

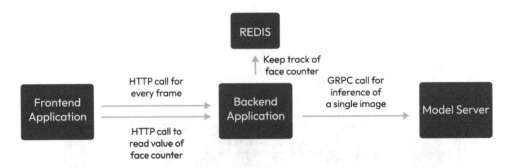

Figure 7.13 – Inferencing application architecture

The inferencing application consists of two parts. The first is a simple HTML5 application that captures the feed from your video camera and sends the frames to the backend application. The backend application then receives the data via HTTPS, transforms the received frame into a format that our model accepts, and makes an inference call. The backend application also connects to the Redis cache and increments a counter whenever a face is detected from our model response.

The backend application exposes another HTTP endpoint from where you can receive the current counter value from the Redis cache. Similarly, the frontend application queries the counter value and displays the counter on the web page.

Let's look into the code for these components. We will start by looking at how the frontend application is sending the frames it captured from your local video camera and sending the captured frames to the backend. The full code for the frontend application can be found in chapter7/serve-model/capture-video.html. It uses the HTML5 canvas element to draw the captured frame from the video camera and the HTML5 video element to capture the stream from the camera. The takepicture function performs the video capture and display on the canvas, as shown below. After capturing the current frame, the takepicture function makes an AJAX call for the backend service. Make sure to point to the right route for your backend service here. Do note that the code is using the JavaScript btoa function to convert the image into a Base64-encoded ASCII string before sending it over the HTTPS channel:

```
function takepicture() {
var context = canvas.getContext('2d');
if (width && height) {
canvas.width = width;
canvas.height = height;
context.drawImage(video, 0, 0, width, height);
var imgData = context.getImageData(0, 0, width,\
    height).data;
var data = canvas.toDataURL('image/png');
```

```
photo.setAttribute('src', data);
$.ajax({
url: 'https://face-detection-app-wines.apps.fmflask2.faisallabs.net/
infer',
type: 'POST',
data: btoa(imgData),
dataType: 'text',
async: true,
contentType: 'application/text; charset=utf-8'
});
} else {
clearphoto();
}
}
```

In the same file, the refreshFaceCounter function performs another AJAX call to get the value of the counter from the application and update the value on the web page. As mentioned earlier, make sure that you are using the right URL for your backend service on this page. The refreshFaceCounter code is shown here:

```
function refreshFaceCounter(){
$.ajax({
url: 'https://face-detection-app-      wines.apps.fmflask2.faisallabs.
net/infer-count',
type: 'GET',
async: true,
success: function (result) {
document.getElementById('counter').textContent = result;
},
});
}
```

Next is the backend code. The code is available in the chapter7/serve-model/app.py file. The backend code uses Python and its aiohttp library to build two REST endpoints. The first one is at /infer, which is captured in the infer function in the code. You can see it is quite simple code that just makes a call to perform inference and increment the Redis counter when a face is detected and returns a response:

```
@routes.post('/infer')
async def infer(request: Request) -> Response:
max_confidence_index = await infer_request(request)
#2 is face
if max_confidence_index == 2:
await increment_face_counter()
return web.Response(text=str(max_confidence_index))
```

The `infer_request` function performs an actual inference with the deployed server on Red Hat OpenShift Data Science. It first converts the received image from the frontend, which is in the RGBA format, to RGB. Our model is trained on RGB, and this conversion is required because the model expects the 256,256,3 shape for the input. Note that the following snippet is not the full function; you can get the complete code from the associated GitHub repository for this book:

```
async def infer_request(request) -> bool:
raw_frame = await request.read()
decoded_frame = base64.b64decode(raw_frame).decode()
values = [int(i) for i in decoded_frame.split(',')]
image_width = 255 * 4
image_frame:int = np.zeros((256, 256, 3), dtype=np.float32)
for i in range(0, 256):
for j in range (0, 256):
firstitem = (i * (image_width)) + (j * 4)
image_frame[i][j][0] = np.float32(values[firstitem])
image_frame[i][j][1] = np.float32(values[firstitem+1])
image_frame[i][j][2] = np.float32(values[firstitem+2])

video_frame = image_frame.reshape(1, 256, 256, 3)
.

.
```

The other endpoint of the backend is the one that listens on the `/infer-count` URL and returns the current value of the face counter. You can see the full function in the following code snippet. It uses the Python `redis` library to make calls for the Redis server:

```
@routes.get('/infer-count')
async def get_infer_count(request: Request) -> Response:
redis = app[REDIS_CLIENT]
value = await redis.get('face-count')
print(f"Infer Count ->{value}")
return web.Response(text=value)
```

The code also defines the location of the model and the Redis server at the beginning of the file. Make sure that the internal OpenShift service names are available before you deploy this code. Look at the following two lines, where the URL of the model and the Redis server are defined. As you see in the code, you can override them by defining the correct environment variable in your OpenShift deployments:

```
MODEL_SERVER = os.getenv('MODEL_SERVER', \
    'modelmesh-serving.wines.svc.cluster.local:8033')
REDIS_SERVER = os.getenv('REDIS_SERVER', \
    'redis://redis.wines.svc.cluster.local:6379')
```

Deploying the inferencing application

OpenShift not only provides easy model development and deployment but also works smoothly for deploying and running your inferencing application, as you will see in this section.

Navigate to the **Developer** view of the OpenShift platform, which provides a workflow for developer use cases, such as deploying a Python application, in our case. Click on the dropdown just below the hamburger menu on the left-hand side of the OpenShift console and you will get two options. The first is **Administrator** and the second is **Developer**, as shown in *Figure 7.14*.

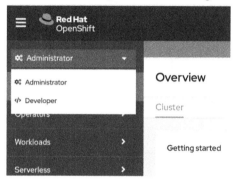

Figure 7.14 – OpenShift Developer view

Click on the **Developer** option and you will be taken to the OpenShift **Developer** view. The view is shown in the following figure, with the **face-detection** project selected in the **Project** dropdown in the right pane. Click on the **Add** button on the left. You will be presented with different options from where an application can be deployed.

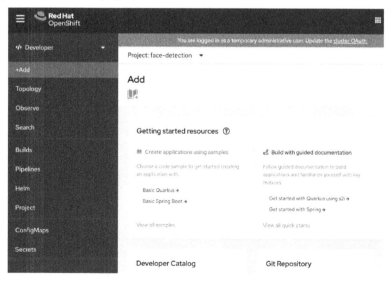

Figure 7.15 – OpenShift Developer importing application from Git

Select the **Import from Git** option because the backend Python application you have built is available in the Git repository of this book. You will be presented with the screen in *Figure 7.16*, where you specify how and where your application will be deployed.

We want you to stop here and consider how easy it is to package and deploy an application on the OpenShift platform. You just point to your code, and the platform will containerize, deploy, and expose your application automatically.

The first section of the **Import from Git** screen shown in *Figure 7.16* contains the location of the Git repository and **Context dir**, which is an optional folder name where your application resides in the repository. The `Context dir` value would be `chapter7/serve-model`.

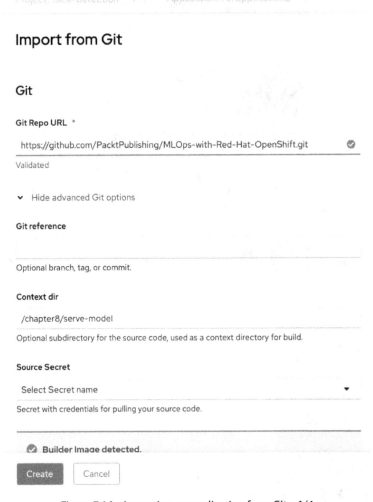

Figure 7.16 – Importing an application from Git – 1/4

The second part of this screen shows the automatic detection of the application stack. Notice that the code repository could be of any stack, such as Java, Go, or Python. OpenShift automatically detects the code repository and gives you the option to make any changes, such as the Python image, which mentions the version of Python OpenShift will use. If your required version is not available, you can create your own builder image; however, creating builder images is beyond the scope of this book.

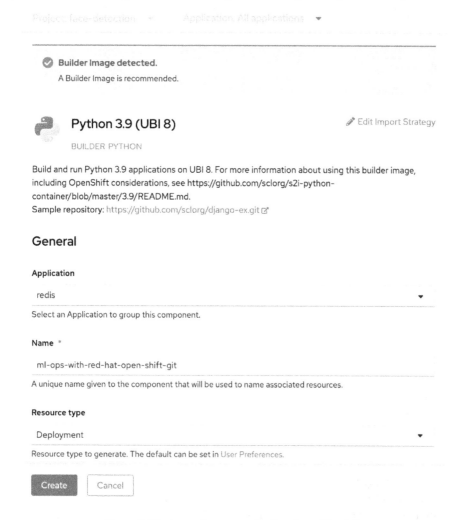

Figure 7.17 – Importing an application from Git – 2/4

The third section of the **Import from Git** screen is where you input a name for your application. The **Add pipeline** checkbox, if checked (we recommend that you do check it) tells OpenShift to create a deployment pipeline for further deployment of your application.

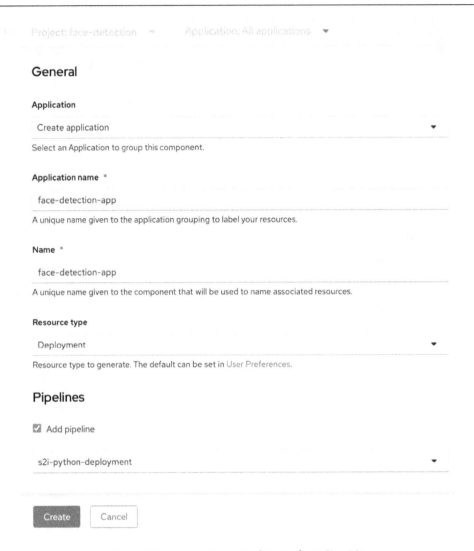

Figure 7.18 – Importing an application from Git – 3/4

The last section of the **Import from Git** screen is where you mention the port on which your application is listening, which is 8080 in our case. You also check the **Create a route** box, which will create a new OpenShift route, and your application will be accessible from outside the OpenShift cluster. The last checkbox, **Secure Route**, will make the route **Secure Socket Layer** (**SSL**) enabled and the traffic from the client computer up to the OpenShift cluster will be encrypted. Disable the **Secure Route** checkbox to make the setup easier, especially if your OpenShift cluster does not have a valid route certificate from a certificate authority. However, for production, you should always make it secure. Now, hit the **Create** button, and this will package and deploy the Python application from the Git repository to OpenShift.

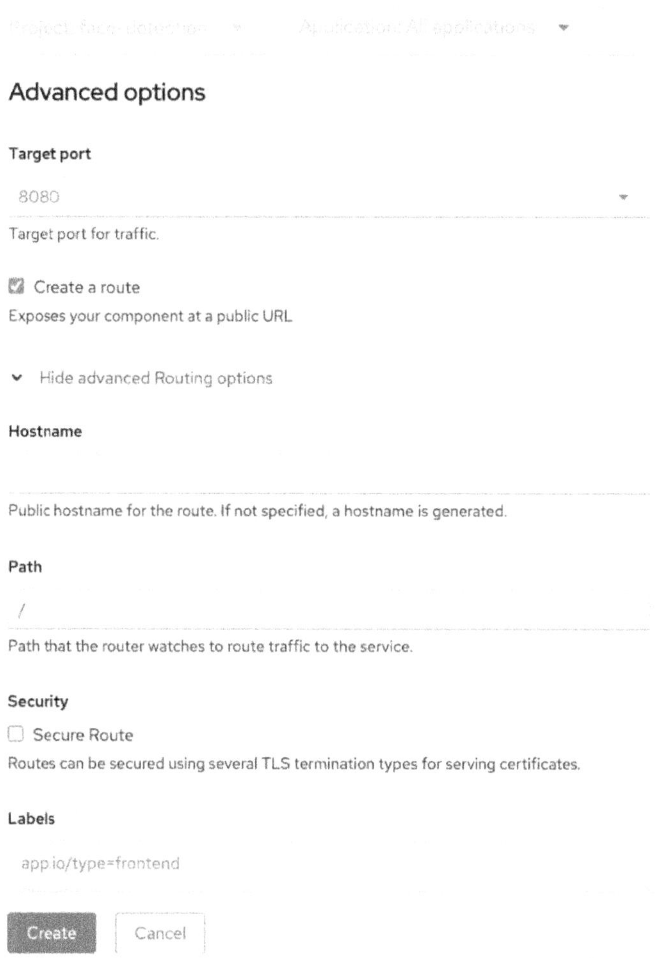

Project: face-detection   ▼   Application: All applications   ▼

Advanced options

Target port

8080   ▼

Target port for traffic.

☑ Create a route
Exposes your component at a public URL

▼ Hide advanced Routing options

Hostname

Public hostname for the route. If not specified, a hostname is generated.

Path

/

Path that the router watches to route traffic to the service.

Security

☐ Secure Route
Routes can be secured using several TLS termination types for serving certificates.

Labels

app.io/type=frontend

[Create]   [Cancel]

Figure 7.19 – Importing an application from Git – 4/4

Whoa! That's a lot of setup and configuration required to run our application, and thanks to OpenShift, all of this can be done on a single screen. The value of OpenShift should be clear to you now, after you have seen how it provides a complete platform for both your ML and application requirements.

The OpenShift platform will automatically start the first run of the deployment pipeline. You can see the progress of the pipeline by going to the OpenShift console, selecting **Pipelines**, and finding the **pipeline-face-detection** pipeline. You will get a screen like the one in *Figure 7.20*, where you can see the progress of the pipeline.

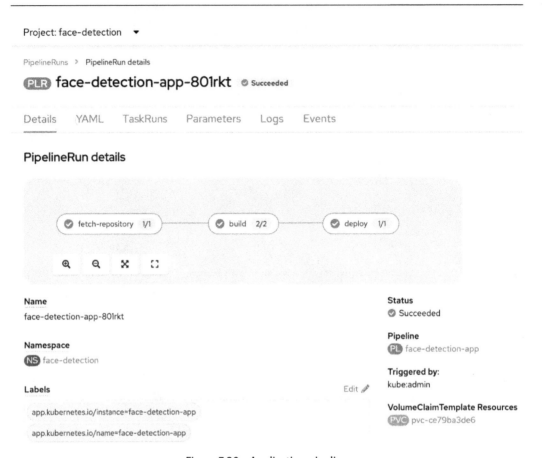

Figure 7.20 – Application pipeline

After the pipeline is successful, verify that the application is up and running. You can validate the application state by going to the OpenShift developer console and searching for the app name; in this example, it is face. You will see a screen similar to the one shown in *Figure 7.21*. Note that you may have named the application something different; be sure to search for the correct name.

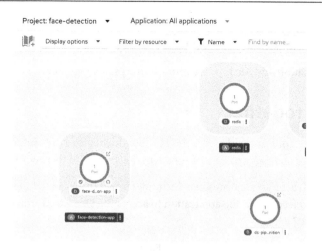

Figure 7.21 – Application deployed – Developer view

The next step is to select the **face-detection-app** application from the topology view. To do so, find the route URL from the right panel. In this example, it is **face-detection-app,** as seen in *Figure 7.22*.

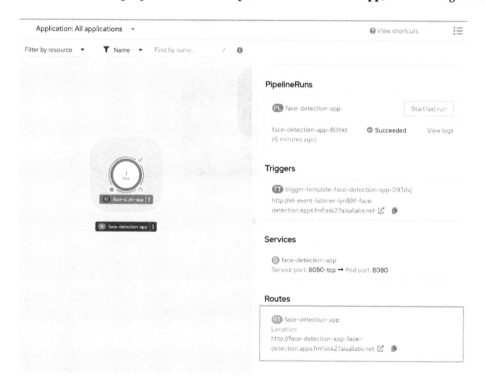

Figure 7.22 – Application's OpenShift route

From this screen, you can get the URL of your **face-detection-app** application. Use this URL to replace the URLs used in the `capture-video.html` frontend HTML file in the book repository.

Now, let's run the application and see how we bring all the pieces together.

Bringing it all together

Start with updating the frontend code with the HTTP address for **face-detection-app** as in the `refreshFaceCounter` and `takepicture` functions. Keep in mind that your URL will be different.

Save and load the HTML file into your browser. The browser will throw a warning that the application is trying to capture video feed; allow the application to access the video feed. You will get a screen like the one shown in *Figure 7.23*.

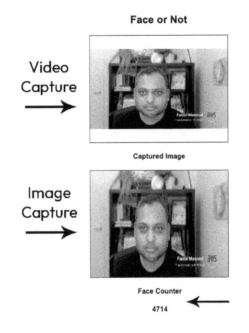

Figure 7.23 – Application UI capturing video and inferencing

The web page captures the video stream from your laptop camera and displays it in the top area of the page. The middle area shows the image capture every 250 milliseconds as configured on the web page, and the bottom counter displays the number of images captured.

You will notice that the counter is continuously incremented while the person sits in front of the camera. This means that every 250 milliseconds, an image has been captured and sent to the inference backend service that applies the model and updates the counter in the Redis server. Another call from your browser fetches the current count and displays it.

Now, the second test is to put your hand in front of the camera, as shown in *Figure 7.24*, and you will notice that the counter stops being incremented. This is because the model does not detect any face in the image, so it does not increment the counter. You can also stop the counter by putting your finger in front of the camera. Remember when you train the model that it detects a human finger, too, and because it is not a face, it does not increase the count.

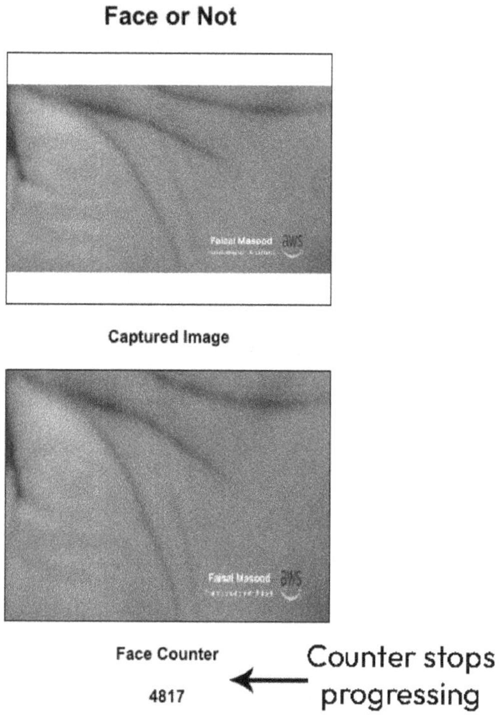

Figure 7.24 – Application UI capturing video and inferencing

As an exercise, you can increase the image capture from every 250 milliseconds to every 50 milliseconds and observe how the load increases on your inferencing application. You can use OpenShift's horizontal scaling capabilities to scale not only the application but the model too to serve more load as it comes.

As you can see, there are many components involved in training and deploying your model, and each component requires a different infrastructure to run. The last topic we will cover is how you can use OpenShift's autoscaling capabilities to optimize the running cost for your teams.

Optimizing cost for your ML platform

In this section, you will learn how to use different OpenShift capabilities with Red Hat Data Science to optimize the cost for your platform. While we will not dive deep into this topic, we will provide you with some basic concepts to continue optimizing your platform resources.

When you run any software on the Red Hat OpenShift platform, such as a Jupyter notebook, build pipelines, and model serving, all of it runs as containers on the platform. These containers run on the machines or worker nodes, which could be a VM in a cloud platform such as Amazon EC2. Let's see how OpenShift provisions machines to run containers for your MLOps needs.

Machine management in OpenShift

Machine management is OpenShift's capability to work with the cloud or on-premises infrastructure providers, such as **Amazon Web Services** (**AWS**) or **VMware** (**VMW**), and to provision and scale the machines for your workloads. OpenShift adapts to changing workloads via machine management capabilities. As mentioned, the details of this capability are beyond the scope of this book, but we will explain the basic concepts through which you can control the cost of your cluster.

Machine management is implemented as a set of **CustomResourceDefinitions** (**CRDs**). The following are the most important CRDs for machine management:

- `Machine`: Specifies the configuration of each node of your cluster. You can see the number of machines in your cluster by running the following command:

   ```
   oc get machines -n openshift-machine-api
   ```

- `MachineSet`: Think of it as the deployment object for Pods. You define how many Pods you desire in the deployment object. Like it, `MachineSet` specifies the desired number of machine resources to maintain. You can have a different `MachineSet` object for different resources, such as a `MachineSet` object with GPUs or a `MachineSet` object in a particular availability zone of the cloud provider. You can run the following command to see all the `MachineSet` objects in your cluster:

   ```
   oc get machineset -n openshift-machine-api
   ```

- `MachineAutoscaler`: This object is associated with the `MachineSet` object. You define the minimum and maximum scaling boundaries for your `Machine` in a specific `MachineSet` resource, and the autoscaler keeps the `Machine` in the defined range.

- `ClusterAutoscaler`: This object helps you manage autoscaling policies such as cluster-wide minimum and maximum resources such as cores, memory, and GPU. You can define a scaling policy to, for example, just scale up and never scale down.

Now, let's see how these objects work together to provide a dynamic infrastructure for your platform.

This `ClusterAutoscaler` object watches for the Pods that the Kubernetes scheduler is unable to schedule on any of the existing nodes. After detecting a shortage of resources, it works with the `MachineAutoscaler` object, which then scales the `MachineSet` object state up or down based on the policy. The following diagram captures the workings of the **Dynamic Machine Management (DMM)** capabilities of the OpenShift platform.

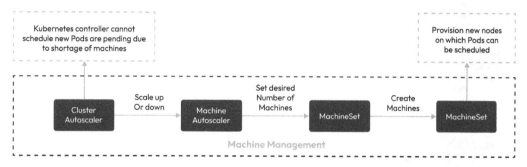

Figure 7.25 – OpenShift machine management

So, the first cost optimization strategy is to use machine management with dynamic scaling to add and remove machines as the load fluctuates. When you define a pod for inference, when the request comes in, OpenShift can add more machines, and when the traffic spike is gone, OpenShift will automatically remove the machines, saving your infrastructure cost on the cloud provider.

DMM is such a critical topic that AWS has created its own open source project called **Karpenter** (`https://karpenter.sh`), which provides another way of dynamically provisioning nodes for your cluster. Because Karpenter is specific to AWS, it can provision machines faster than `ClusterAutoscaler`. Consider Karpenter if you are running your OpenShift platform on AWS infrastructure.

Automatically shutting down a notebook

You have seen that `ClusterAutoscaler` can scale up and down the nodes based on the Pods' scheduling requests. For inferencing, the Pods can come and go based on the load, but the platform also provides Jupyter notebooks for your data scientists and engineers to build models and process data. These notebooks can be quite taxing on resources such as memory and GPU. How can you optimize the resources when the notebook is not being used by the team? Red Hat OpenShift Data Science provides an automatic shutdown of the notebook if it is idle for a specific set of time. Note that OpenShift will only stop the machine and keep the data safe so the team can start where they left off. You can find the settings in the left-hand menu of the OpenShift Data Science dashboard, as shown in *Figure 7.26*.

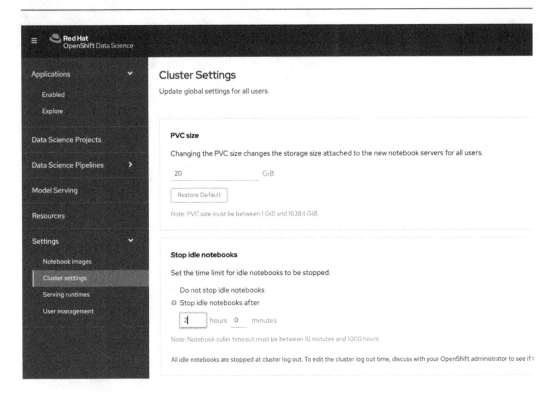

Figure 7.26 – Automatic shutdown of notebooks

The second strategy is to make sure that the notebooks are configured to stop after a certain time.

Spot Instances

Spot Instances or **Spot virtual machines** (**Spot VMs**) are unused capacities in a cloud provider data center. All three major vendors provide Spot VMs. For example, in AWS, a Spot Instance comes with a discount of up to 90% compared to On-Demand Instances. However, the cloud vendor might terminate a Spot Instance at any time when the resources are needed for someone else, so this type of instance is for stateless and fault-tolerant workloads only.

Now, imagine that you are running production models and you want to use the Spot capability. One way is to run the minimum number of model servers on normal instances and scale on Spot Instances. Say you want to run 10 Pods of your model with a minimum availability of 2 Pods. So, the remaining 8 Pods can run on Spot Instances, and with OpenShift machine management, when the cloud provider takes the instances back, OpenShift will provision a new one. You can achieve this by creating two different `MachineSet` objects, one machine set for the normal instances and one machine set for the Spot Instances. The autoscaler for normal machine sets will have a small number of machines, while the Spot autoscaler would have a larger number to scale to.

Let's see what a machine set looks like. Go to the OpenShift console and select the **MachineSets** menu option under the **Compute** section. You will see multiple machine sets there, as shown in *Figure 7.27*.

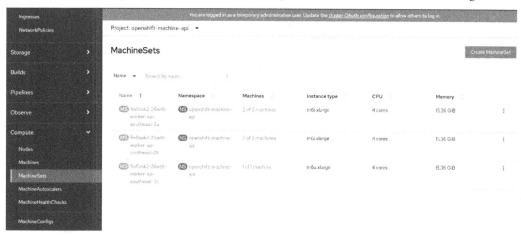

Figure 7.27 – Machine sets

Click on the machine set of your choosing and then select the **YAML** tab as shown in the following figure. You can see the `spec.metadata.labels` field at line number 126 defines the labels that will be allocated to the nodes created through this machine set.

Figure 7.28 – Machine sets

Now that the nodes have been labeled, next you have to tell your inference Pods to use the machines. OpenShift Data Science allows you to use Kubernetes node selection or node toleration capabilities on your model inference Pods. Go to your Red Hat Data Science **wines** project and find out the models deployed by clicking on the **Deploy model** options as shown in *Figure 7.29*.

Figure 7.29 – Deployed models view

You see that there are four models deployed in my cluster. Let's pick one model, say **wine**, and see how we can add a node selector to it so it goes to the machines we provision for the model. I picked the deployed model named **wine**. There is a specific Kubernetes `InferenceService` object that defines the Red Hat Data Science instance, and we need to change the definition to use the custom node with specific labels.

Run the following command with the right model name as per your environment to see whether the object is there:

```
oc get inferenceservice/wine -n wines
```

You will see the following output:

```
$oc get inferenceservice/wine -n wines
NAME    URL                                          READY    PREV    LATEST    PREVROLLE
wine    grpc://modelmesh-serving.wines:8033          True
```

Figure 7.30 – Deployed model as InferenceService

Next we edit this model service and add the node selector as follows. First, run the following command to bring up the resource in edit mode:

```
oc edit inferenceservice/wine -n wines
```

This command will open the yaml object in an editor as shown in *Figure 7.31*. Add the node selector key as provided in the screenshot in *Figure 7.31*, just after the spec.predictor key.

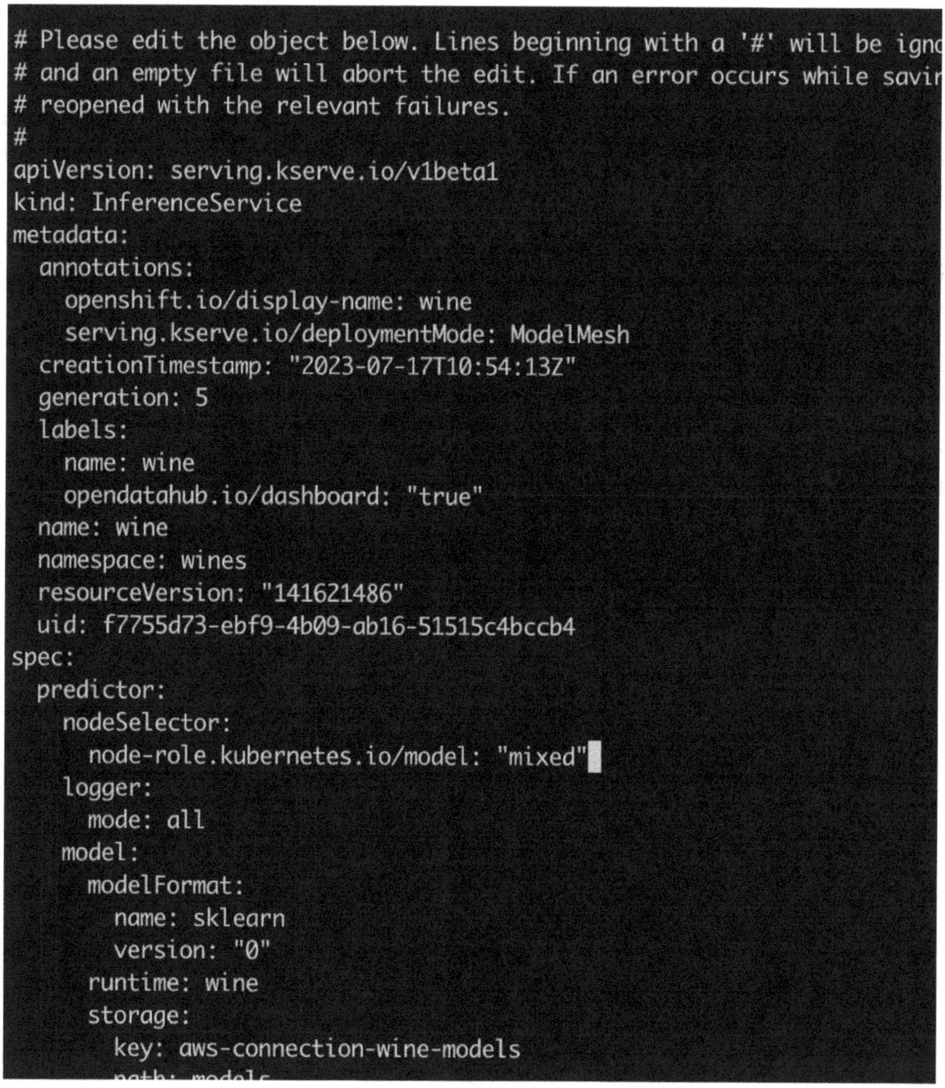

```
# Please edit the object below. Lines beginning with a '#' will be ign
# and an empty file will abort the edit. If an error occurs while savi
# reopened with the relevant failures.
#
apiVersion: serving.kserve.io/v1beta1
kind: InferenceService
metadata:
  annotations:
    openshift.io/display-name: wine
    serving.kserve.io/deploymentMode: ModelMesh
  creationTimestamp: "2023-07-17T10:54:13Z"
  generation: 5
  labels:
    name: wine
    opendatahub.io/dashboard: "true"
  name: wine
  namespace: wines
  resourceVersion: "141621486"
  uid: f7755d73-ebf9-4b09-ab16-51515c4bccb4
spec:
  predictor:
    nodeSelector:
      node-role.kubernetes.io/model: "mixed"
    logger:
      mode: all
    model:
      modelFormat:
        name: sklearn
        version: "0"
      runtime: wine
      storage:
        key: aws-connection-wine-models
        path: models
```

Figure 7.31 – Deploying inferencing to specific nodes

You can perform all these changes from the OpenShift UI, too. This way, you can control the nodes or machines where your model will be hosted. And with the machine coming from a Spot, you can optimize the cost as per your requirements.

In this section, you have seen multiple ways to optimize the cost and how easy OpenShift and Red Hat OpenShift Data Science make applying these savings.

Summary

Congratulations! You have just experienced building an end-to-end MLOps workflow from scratch. You have trained and deployed an ML model and built a pipeline to automate your model training and deployment workflow using the tools that come with OpenShift Data Science. You have also successfully built a backend application that hosts your model and exposes it as an HTTP endpoint.

You have seen how OpenShift not only provides a full ML life cycle but also hosts your application and supports technologies such as Redis. All the components that have been deployed will benefit from the scalability of the platform.

Your journey does not stop here. The models we have shown here are just an example. You can deploy open source **large language models (LLMs)** on the platform.

Happy learning!

Index

packtpub.com

Subscribe to our online digital library for full access to over 7,000 books and videos, as well as industry leading tools to help you plan your personal development and advance your career. For more information, please visit our website.

Why subscribe?

- Spend less time learning and more time coding with practical eBooks and Videos from over 4,000 industry professionals

- Improve your learning with Skill Plans built especially for you

- Get a free eBook or video every month

- Fully searchable for easy access to vital information

- Copy and paste, print, and bookmark content

Did you know that Packt offers eBook versions of every book published, with PDF and ePub files available? You can upgrade to the eBook version at packtpub.com and as a print book customer, you are entitled to a discount on the eBook copy. Get in touch with us at customercare@packtpub.com for more details.

At www.packtpub.com, you can also read a collection of free technical articles, sign up for a range of free newsletters, and receive exclusive discounts and offers on Packt books and eBooks.

Other Books You May Enjoy

If you enjoyed this book, you may be interested in these other books by Packt:

Engineering MLOps - Second Edition

Emmanuel Raj

ISBN: 978-1-80323-732-9

- Deploy ML models from the lab environment to production and customize solutions to fit your infrastructure and on-premises needs
- Run ML models on Azure and on devices, including mobile phones and specialized hardware
- Design a streaming service for inference in real-time with Apache Flink
- Explore deployment techniques: A/B testing, phased rollouts, and shadow deployments
- Formulate data governance strategies and pipelines for ML training and deployment

Serverless Machine Learning with Amazon Redshift ML

Debu Panda, Phil Bates, Bhanu Pittampally, Sumeet Joshi

ISBN: 978-1-80461-928-5

- Utilize Redshift Serverless for data ingestion, data analysis, and machine learning
- Create supervised and unsupervised models and learn how to supply your own custom parameters
- Discover how to use time series forecasting in your data warehouse
- Create a SageMaker endpoint and use that to build a Redshift ML model for remote inference
- Find out how to operationalize machine learning in your data warehouse
- Use model explainability and calculate probabilities with Amazon Redshift ML

Packt is searching for authors like you

If you're interested in becoming an author for Packt, please visit `authors.packtpub.com` and apply today. We have worked with thousands of developers and tech professionals, just like you, to help them share their insight with the global tech community. You can make a general application, apply for a specific hot topic that we are recruiting an author for, or submit your own idea.

Share Your Thoughts

Now you've finished *MLOps with Red Hat OpenShift*, we'd love to hear your thoughts! Scan the QR code below to go straight to the Amazon review page for this book and share your feedback or leave a review on the site that you purchased it from.

`https://packt.link/r/1-805-12023-9`

Your review is important to us and the tech community and will help us make sure we're delivering excellent quality content.

Download a free PDF copy of this book

Thanks for purchasing this book!

Do you like to read on the go but are unable to carry your print books everywhere?

Is your eBook purchase not compatible with the device of your choice?

Don't worry, now with every Packt book you get a DRM-free PDF version of that book at no cost.

Read anywhere, any place, on any device. Search, copy, and paste code from your favorite technical books directly into your application.

The perks don't stop there, you can get exclusive access to discounts, newsletters, and great free content in your inbox daily

Follow these simple steps to get the benefits:

1. Scan the QR code or visit the link below

https://packt.link/free-ebook/9781805120230

2. Submit your proof of purchase
3. That's it! We'll send your free PDF and other benefits to your email directly

www.ingramcontent.com/pod-product-compliance
Lightning Source LLC
Chambersburg PA
CBHW080639060326
40690CB00021B/4996